MW00614428

ENCOUNTERING GOD'S NORMAL

ENCOUNTERING GOD'S NORMAL

ELEVATING YOUR UNDERSTANDING OF
YOUR HEAVENLY FATHER'S DOMAIN

DR. KEVIN L. ZADAI

Unless otherwise indicated, Scripture quotations are taken from the New King James Version. Copyright © 1982 by Thomas Nelson, Inc. Used by permission. All rights reserved.

All Scripture quotations marked (KJV) are taken from the King James Version. Public Domain.

Scripture quotations marked (NLT) are taken from the Holy Bible, New Living Translation, copyright ©1996, 2004, 2015 by Tyndale House Foundation. Used by permission of Tyndale House Publishers, a Division of Tyndale House Ministries, Carol Stream, Illinois 60188. All rights reserved.

Scripture quotations marked (AMP) are taken from the Amplified Bible, Copyright © 1954, 1958, 1962, 1964, 1965, 1987 by The Lockman Foundation. Used by permission. www.Lockman.org.

Scripture quotations marked (TPT) are from The Passion Translation®. Copyright © 2017, 2018 by Passion & Fire Ministries, Inc. Used by permission. All rights reserved. www.thePassionTranslation.com.

Please note that Warrior Notes publishing style capitalizes certain pronouns in Scripture that refer to the Father, Son, and Holy Spirit, which may differ from some publishers' styles. Take note that the name "satan" and related names are not capitalized. We choose not to acknowledge him, even to the point of violating accepted grammatical rules. All emphasis within Scripture quotations is the author's own.

Cover design: Virtually Possible Designs
Editing by Lisa Thompson at www.writebylisa.com
For more information about our school, go to
www.warriornotesschool.com. Reach us on the internet:
www.Kevinzadai.com

ISBN 13 TP: 978-1-6631-0002-3

Dedication

I dedicate this book to the Lord Jesus Christ. When I died during surgery and met with Jesus on the other side, He insisted that I return to life on earth and that I help people discover their destinies. Because of Jesus's love and concern for people, the Lord has actually chosen to send a person back from death to help everyone who will receive that help so that his or her destiny and purpose are secure in Him. I want You, Lord, to know that when you come to take me to be with You someday, I sincerely hope that people remember not me but the revelation of Jesus Christ through me. I want others to know that I am merely obeying Your heavenly calling and mission, which is to reveal Your plan for the fulfillment of the divine destiny for each of God's children.

Acknowledgments

In addition to sharing my story with everyone through the book *Heavenly Visitation: A Guide to the Supernatural,* God has commissioned me to write over fifty books and study guides. Most recently, the Lord gave me the commission to produce this book, *Encountering God's Normal.* This book addresses some of the revelations concerning the areas that Jesus reviewed and revealed to me through the Word of God and by the Spirit of God during several visitations. I want to thank everyone who has encouraged me, assisted me, and prayed for me during the writing of this work, especially my spiritual parents, Dr. Jesse Duplantis and Dr. Cathy Duplantis. Special thanks to my wonderful wife, Kathi, for her love and dedication to the Lord and me. Thank you to a great staff for the wonderful job editing this book. Special thanks as well to all my friends who know about *Encountering God's Normal* and how to operate in this for the next move of God's Spirit!

Contents

Introduction

When I encountered Jesus in the heavenly realms in 1992, I realized several truths that have changed me forever. First, the heavenly kingdom is perfect in every way. Second, I saw that God's initial intention for man and this earth was also perfection. We are His children, and we were destined to live on the earth forever in that godly perfection.

I have, over the years, seen the body of Christ moving toward this final hour in history where the culmination of all the ages is approaching. In this final hour, "For the earnest expectation of the creature waiteth for the manifestation of the sons of God" (Romans 8:19).

I saw the throne room and the innumerable presence of saints worshipping the Lamb who was on the throne. I saw in an instant that this gathering was our heavenly Father's goal: to redeem His family back to Himself. At this point, I encountered God's normal. His ways are definitely higher than our ways. "For just as the heavens are higher than the earth, so my ways are higher than your ways, and my thoughts higher than your thoughts" (Isaiah 55:9).

Now, I present to you this amazing study on the understanding that was imparted to me by the Word of God and this amazing glimpse into our immediate future. Enjoy!

Kevin L. Zadai
Founder and President of Warrior Notes and Warrior Notes School of Ministry

CHAPTER 1

AWAKENING TO GOD'S NORMAL

Ask, and it will be given to you; seek, and you will find;
knock, and it will be opened to you.
—Matthew 7:7

E ncountering God's normal will eventually become normal to you. It may be shocking when you see God's personality and how He truly thinks. It will be revolutionary when you hear His voice and when He says something to you that you had never thought of before or when you realize that you actually had access to it all along. And how amazing it will be when you receive something from God that you didn't think you could ever have, and His response to you will be, "Well, it's already at your door." It's as if Amazon just left you a delivery. Angels are delivering packages to your house, but you need to answer the door.

At this point, we are waiting on Jesus to come back, and He is waiting on us. This is why nothing is happening in our churches anymore because we're both waiting on each other. Why are we waiting on God? Hasn't He already said, "Ask, and you shall receive, seek and you shall find, knock and the door shall be opened to you?" In Matthew 8:3, Jesus told the man with leprosy that His will *is* to heal! If you are waiting on Jesus to do something else for you to be healed, you are missing it. Do you believe Jesus when He says, "All things are possible to him who believes" (Mark 9:23)? Jesus is throwing it right back at us. We must believe—even on our deathbed, we never give up. That is how Jesus and His disciples preached, and they were killed for preaching it.

The Holy Spirit Is the Spirit of Truth

These things I have written to you concerning those who try to deceive you. But the anointing which you have received from Him abides in you, and you do not need that anyone teach you; but as the same anointing teaches you concerning all things, and is true, and is not a lie, and just as it has taught you, you will abide in Him. (1 John 2:26–27)

If you listen to teaching outside of God's Word, you will not know what you believe anymore. God has provided all that you need to discern the truth. You have your Bible and the Spirit of God—the Teacher, who is living inside you. The Holy Spirit bears witness with you if what's being said is the truth or not.

First John was written to born-again believers, and in chapter 2, the author addresses the false doctrine circulating among them. He wanted Spirit-filled believers to understand that the anointing we have received from the Holy One abides in us and we do not need anyone to teach us.

This type of teaching is not referring to the fivefold office of a teacher; if it were, it would result in a contradiction between the office of a teacher and the Spirit of Truth. The office of teacher is one of the five offices that God established for the edification of the body of Christ as outlined in Ephesians 4. The role of the Spirit of Truth is to reveal and enable us to combat false doctrine.

You may notice a hybrid group of people who have come into the church portraying themselves as believers, but they are not true believers. We know this because they have no fruit. They are clouds without rain. Paul describes these unbelieving believers as having a form of godliness but denying the power of God (2 Timothy 3:5).

God's Power Is Alive within Us

Anyone who claims to be a Christian and denies the power of God is not a true Christian. Paul preached Christ and His crucifixion because that is all he knew. He knew about the resurrection and the fact that Jesus was raised from the dead. The resurrection is truly the power that we believe in (Romans 8:11); it is our hope. Jesus died, but we don't stop there. When we acknowledge that we have the same power inside us that raised Jesus from the dead, we will walk, live, and demonstrate that same power in our lives.

> Then He spoke many things to them in parables, saying, "Behold, a sower went out to sow. And as he sowed, some seed fell by the wayside; and the birds came and devoured them. Some fell on stony places, where they did not have much earth, and they immediately sprang up because they had no depth of earth. But when the sun was up, they were scorched,

and because they had no root, they withered away. And some fell among thorns, and the thorns sprang up and choked them. But others fell on good ground and yielded a crop: some a hundredfold, some sixty, some thirty. He who has ears to hear, let him hear!" (Matthew 13:3–9)

Becoming Like Jesus Is God's Normal

When God speaks, if you will take the seed of the Word into your heart, the soil within your heart will start to reproduce the Word until it grows and multiplies into a crop, and that's when it starts to change you. When this begins to happen, people will know you by your fruit; they will no longer know you as the person you were before. As this happens, your personality will begin to change, and you will become more and more like God. You will become like Jesus and begin to act like Him (Romans 8:29). You will start to make decisions like He did because you will leave your old ways. You will make the right decisions even if it hurts. You will then begin to live in God's normal for your life.

In Matthew 13:3–9, Jesus explained that when the Word is sown, different types of soil receive it. In this parable, only

25 percent of the soil was expected to produce a crop. I don't know about you, but I do not want just a 25 percent result— I want 100 percent! I'm not talking about just the one-quarter getting the hundred-fold; I want to prepare hearts so that all four soils converge into the one good soil. As I preach the good news of the gospel, I'm taking out the thorns and the stones. As the Word is received, it is getting rid of the cares of this life and the deceitfulness of riches. I'm getting rid of all that stuff, and a migration then occurs.

Jesus explained that a migration out of the religious system is occurring right now. People are no longer satisfied with religion; they seek to join a body of believers where the Word of God is preached with signs and wonders following. Signs and wonders are not specific to just any one individual. Only One is our head, and His name is Jesus. His body is to be one. We have one head, and we have one body with many members (1 Corinthians 12).

"Things are moving fast, and if you want to walk in the Spirit, you must always be ready to listen and obey God."

We need to understand that events are moving at a fast pace right now. If you want to walk in the Spirit, you must be ready to listen to God. When He speaks, you must know that the next thing that will happen is manifestation. I'm currently in jet flight training, and jets are a lot faster than the planes I've ever flown. In a jet, everything is going at a fast pace. When I move the gear lever down, I expect to instantly hear the gear physically coming down and receive three simultaneous green lights. If that does not happen, then I immediately know I have a problem. All these actions are occurring in an instant because I am traveling four and five hundred miles an hour. Events are moving so fast, and we must walk at this pace in the Spirit. If you want to walk in the Spirit, you must always be ready to listen and immediately obey God. Why? Because it's a war down here, and our lack of response can cause delays. We must be aware that we sometimes cause the delay.

Living in God's Normal Requires a Change of Mindset

You and I are commanders in the Lord's army. When Jesus speaks to you, you are to implement what He says, period. You can see where we don't always have an edge in this area. If you are wondering what you'll do next while flying a jet traveling five hundred miles an hour and you delay taking the next step, within seconds, the cities below you will pass by, and it will already be too late. When you land, you'll already be in the next state.

Well, doesn't it work the same way when God speaks to us? Think about it. Isn't faith really the same as obedience? Isn't it all about the truth that when God says something, He also means it? It's all about hearing God, but in order to hear Him, you must be in a place to do so.

This is why the media bombards us; it's a strategy to keep us out of the move of God, and then our families start acting up. If you don't take care to create your own boundaries and don't take care to go into the secret place or if you're not available when God wants to talk to you, you will miss it.

What if God wants you to enter the secret place without your phone or any distractions? We must be intentional to pursue Him and, at the same time, know that a war is being waged for our souls. Your spirit is already saved; the war is for the soul. Your soul needs to be transformed by the renewing of your mind through the Word of God so that you can take what God is saying through the Holy Spirit and then manifest it. As your mind is renewed, you begin to make decisions based on what God says and not on what you think. However, you must do your part by being present and available, staying yielded, and in a continual relationship with God for this to occur.

When God starts to hang out with you, you will experience His holiness, and all of a sudden, you will realize the sins that have piled up between you and God. At that moment, you will cry and ask God for forgiveness. I am not referring to the sins that you had before you were saved; you're already forgiven of your past sins. I'm talking about the transgressions, omissions, and commissions.

When I was in college, my roommate and I were in our dorm room, and Jesus walked in unannounced. We both hit the deck. The glory of God was so strong that even the metal frames on our beds bent. My roommate and I both began crying like little babies. Now I was already a Christian, but at the moment, I repented of everything that I had ever done and hadn't done. All of it began coming out of me like a machine gun, like bullets shooting out of my mouth. Why? Because at that moment, any sins that were between Jesus and I came to light, and what was between me and my God—

everything that I had allowed to pile up—I repented of all of it, right then and there.

If you notice the time we're living in, people are coming against the message of repentance because they say, "Well, you've already repented." If that were the case, why did every apostle in the Bible say to make sure that you are in Christ and be careful that you don't find yourself outside? Paul warned the believers about this all the time. We must repent every night when we go to bed so we don't allow sin to pile up and come between God and us.

Jesus is Done with Lukewarmness

In Revelation 3:15–16, Jesus explains that if you are lukewarm, He will spew you out of His mouth. Could you imagine if that were the message on Sunday morning in church? Do you think the offerings would be big, or would people come back to that church? But isn't Jesus the head of the church? When these types of messages are presented, the giving can drop. These messages, even though they're right, are not moneymakers. When did the church become a business; how has it become about money?

Jesus told me that because of the current condition of the body of Christ, He is done with lukewarmness. He told me to tell the people, "I'm done." So I'm telling you right now, Jesus won't tolerate lukewarmness. He wants us to be on fire, and we need to speak and walk in and from the fire of God. When we go to work or the grocery store—wherever we go and whatever we do—we need to operate from the fire of God. When we walk in and from the fire, we will not be lukewarm.

Unity of the Faith

When Jesus gives you the Word, you must be quick to hear and accept it as truth. This is why Jesus said, "If you have ears to hear, hear what the Spirit is saying" (Revelation 2:29). Jesus knew one thing could keep a person from hearing from the Spirit of God: a hardened heart. Jesus addressed this with the Pharisees when He said, "Because of the hardness of your hearts, Moses permitted you to divorce your wives, however from the beginning, it was not so" (Matthew 19:8).

If you receive the Word humbly when God speaks to you and you judge yourself by that Word, then God doesn't have to judge you. You won't need a prophet to come to you and judge you because they're not supposed to do that anyway. Prophets are supposed to build people up. (See 1 Corinthians 14:3.) At times, a prophet or an apostle needs to bring correction, but that pertains to doctrine.

The unity of the faith is not about compromising the truth of the Word so that other denominations will be in unity with us. That's not what I'm talking about. The unity of the faith is about correct belief about what the Word of God says. We are the church; however, we are not acting like the church. We do not need to try to get God to accept us; we are already accepted. Do you hear what I'm saying? You are accepted, and He's already proven it.

Unlimited Access to the River of Life

God came to Cain in person and coached him while he was in a fallen state. He came to Adam and Eve when they were in a fallen state. God came anyway and wanted to talk to them. He wants to speak to you even if you are in a fallen state. God wants you. He wants your mind, He wants your will, and He wants you to be full of the joy that comes from the river of life that flows freely from His throne (Revelation

22:1). I saw this river, and there's even fire in it. It's a river of life, and it wells up within us.

> *"God wants you to be full of the joy that comes from the river of life that flows from His throne."*

Do you know what the most supernatural thing you can do is? To yield to the Spirit and allow the river to come up through you so that you're speaking mysteries, building yourself up in the most holy faith, and remaining in the love of God (Jude 1:20–21). That is how you become like the prophets of old. Wherever you go, you won't have it any other way except God's way. You will bind on the earth, and it will be bound in heaven.

Yielding to the Word Is God's Normal

The last time I checked, this nation was built as a democracy, which means you are the voice. The government is supposed to work for you, according to the Constitution. Have you ever read the Constitution? Have you ever read the Amendments? The government is supposed to protect and serve us. Now we know there are still good police officers, senators, and representatives. There are still good leaders and presidents. But they have been placed in those positions to work for you and to serve and protect you. When you go to the polls, you are supposed to vote for those who will work for you and protect you.

When Jesus came, He bought everything back for you and then gave it to you because He—the Father, Jesus, and the Holy Spirit—is for the people. Ministers are also supposed to be there for the people. How and when did it become about them?

Can we still share this truth in church? Third John 1:2 says, "Beloved, I pray that you may prosper in all things and be in health, just as your soul prospers." This is in the New Testament, and I am telling you, it's part of the benefits that we have access to now. Paul clearly understood the benefits of a life in Christ, and that's why he wrote all his letters.

When you begin encountering God's normal, you will have to change, and the only way you can change is by yielding to the Word of God. Just be sure that you are not listening to teachers who are clouds without rain. If you are waiting for the manifestation to occur from a cloud without rain, it won't happen because they can't produce it. Paul spoke about this when he addressed the Corinthians and said, "My speech and my preaching was not with enticing words of man's wisdom, but in demonstration of the Spirit and of power" (1 Corinthians 2:4 KJV).

The Strategy of the Enemy

The enemy's strategy is to get a demon into leaders and people of influence, such as a mayor, governor, or president. This approach is the hardest hitting as it will yield the most effective results for the enemy, even greater than getting many demons into many people.

If you are a disembodied spirit and you are already going to hell and you know you can never repent, you will want to do the most damage possible because you are upset and mad. And that's what these demon spirits do. They look to find the most effective and impactful approach by targeting the people with the most far-reaching influence on the majority of the people, which will cause many to be derailed. This is why many cities, states, and countries are not blessed; they have not acknowledged the one true God and have elected officials that do not acknowledge Him. This reaches and affects each of us.

In America, we have enough people acknowledging the one true God so that we do not need to worry about judgment coming. By acknowledging God, the righteous are stopping His judgment. Understand that judgment is already upon the wicked because their god is satan, and he is a dictator. Now, think about your city, state, and country, and then think about other countries. Everyone who is not in Christ is already under judgment, and the world has already been judged. In 1 Timothy 5:24, Paul writes, "Some men's sins are clearly evident, preceding them to judgment, but those of some men will follow later." Here, Paul is talking about Christians. For some, their judgment is evident right away. However, for others, it follows them later.

God Has Only Good News

I can tell you that I've come to do God's work, not my own. I am representing Him. He asks me to defend Him to the people because He said that they were being slandered. In May 2020, Jesus stood three feet away from me and spoke to me for five and a half hours. He said, "We are being slandered, and we are not doing any of the things that they are saying because we are good, and we have only good news. We have a good gospel, and we are good. We only do those things that benefit our creation. We want everyone to come to heaven because it is not our desire that anyone should perish. If people die and go to hell, it's because they decided to." The Bible says that no one will be without excuse because even creation testifies of the gospel and testifies that there is a God (Romans 1:20). Jesus explained the whole thing to me. People know there is a God, and they need to seek him.

Right now, Jesus is appearing to Muslims nightly, and those He appears to are being converted. Jesus said to me, "I shouldn't have to do that. You should be doing that." So I ask you, don't you think he's messing with the system by appearing to people? Don't you think the church should be doing this? "But when He, the Spirit of truth, comes, He will guide you into all the truth; for He will not speak on His own initiative, but whatever He hears, He will speak, and He will disclose to you what is to come. He will glorify Me, for He will take of Mine and will disclose it to you" (John 16:13 NIV).

Christians know what is to come because the Bible says that the Holy Spirit guides us into all truth and shows us what is to come. In verse 14, Jesus went on to say, "The Spirit will glorify Me." It doesn't say, "He will glorify the minister, drawing attention to the preacher." Is anyone else on earth teaching this? Think about it—someone must stand up and not be afraid. If people pull their money from my ministry because I am saying these things, I don't care. I will still show up, and I will not be bought. The gospel message will still go forth. The Holy Spirit gave me this declaration, confirming that God will indeed ensure His message goes forth.

Jesus said to the disciples, "But when He, the Spirit of Truth, comes, He will guide you into all the truth . . . He will speak whatever He hears [from the Father—the message regarding the Son], and He will disclose to you what is to come [in the future]" (John 16:13 AMP). He was not addressing this truth only to the fivefold: the prophets, apostles, pastors, teachers, or evangelists. Jesus is talking to the entire body of Christ, to everyone that believes. "He will glorify and honor Me, because He (the Holy Spirit) will take from what is Mine and will disclose it to you" (John 16:14 AMP).

This is what you need to remember. I want you to stay in there with the Lord, no matter how hard it gets, because He has a plan; no matter how bad it looks or how bad it gets, it's just momentary. It's not over until God says it's over. He will have the last word, and He will speak. I am not concerned with what politicians or the media are saying; what I care about is what Jesus is saying and knowing that the Holy Spirit is taking it and giving it to us. That is what I care about. We must keep our focus, no matter what.

Encountering God's Glory

Jesus explained to me that a separation is occurring right now. As a body, God is taking us into a spiritual Goshen. Like the Israelites were protected from the plagues, you will begin to see yourself in a place of protection (Exodus 8:22). If you make the Most High your dwelling place, you will slip into the secret place where every believer is supposed to be anyway (Psalm 91), and from that place, nothing will by any means hurt you. In Luke 10:19, Jesus was quoting from Psalm 91 when He said, "I give you the authority to trample on serpents and scorpions, and over all the power of the enemy, and nothing shall by any means hurt you." God won't come in if you are not living a separate life. That is why He fights for the messages about the fear of the Lord, repentance, and living the crucified life.

Encountering God's normal is when His personality shows up and He shows up in the person of His glory. When the glory hits you, you encounter Him. Jesus came to abide with us forever, and from this point on, it will just get stronger and stronger, and eventually, you won't need me anymore.

When Moses encountered the glory of God, he could hardly stay alive, and God had only walked by him. Moses didn't encounter God face-to-face; God just walked by. Yet even Peter, who had foot-in-the-mouth disease, healed people when his shadow touched them. If Peter can be changed, we can too, and if he were here today, he would testify about how faithful Jesus was in his life and how he finished his race and affected so many and is still impacting us today.

Transformed in His Presence

"We can know the inner workings of what God is doing through our relationship with Jesus."

When you encounter God's normal, it will mean that He has shown up, and He will introduce Himself to you. However, you may no longer be standing when He walks by. You may not even be able to talk anymore. You might walk away from the experience differently. That is called transformation.

Now, Jesus was transformed in front of Peter, James, and John. But Peter misinterpreted what was happening. We do the same thing. Peter thought, *This is good. Maybe I need to build some tents.* But Jesus was just giving them a peek at His pre-existence as God, the pre-existent Christ. That's all He was doing, giving them a glimpse of who He was. He didn't have to do that, but He did. We can know the inner workings of what God is doing through our relationship with Jesus.

John was the one disciple that Jesus loved and trusted more than anyone. But even John said that Jesus didn't commit himself to any man because he knew what was in a man (John 2:24). Jesus knew they would all throw Him under the bus. So he didn't entrust Himself to anyone, but He loved John. Jesus trusted Peter, James, and John the most. However, if you notice, when Jesus raised the dead, He went by Himself. He made everyone leave the room because of unbelief and because even the disciples couldn't handle it. We can all agree that Jesus knew how to get things done, but it meant thinning the herd.

Love Always Pursues the Truth

I will not allow anything that the devil is doing on the earth right now to go unnoticed. I must address this because I want to help equip and prepare the body of Christ. When Jesus was on earth, He told the Pharisees, "You are of your Father, the devil . . . he does not stand in the truth because there is no truth in him. When he speaks a lie, he speaks from his own resources, for he is a liar and the Father of it" (John 8:44). Jesus addressed and confronted the lies when He was on the earth, and we are to follow His example.

The religious system is the devil's system, and no one is brave enough to say that today because they are afraid of losing people in their congregation. But my congregation is the earth, and whoever comes, comes and whoever doesn't, doesn't. I'm talking to the sheep; I'm not talking to goats. I'm talking to wheat; I'm not talking to tares. I'm talking to the wise virgins; I'm not talking to the unwise ones.

God's perfect will for your life is whatever He desires. And He never asked you for your input. He wrote the book about your life before you were born, so He doesn't need you on the board. He made decisions about the human race and everyone that would ever live. He already knows all of them. One of the biggest challenges I face wherever I go is for people to grasp this truth. There is a standard and a metric measurement system. If you have a wrench with a standard measurement and try to use it on a metric lug nut, it won't work. It won't fit your measurement, but God determines the measurement, and He defines the standard. So if your wrench doesn't work, throw it away because it's not about your wrench. It's about the setting on that nut. And God says, "This is the system, and this is the way it will be."

What You Don't Know Is Hurting You

Now, this is the hardest subject I get push back on. You wouldn't believe the pushback I get in the spirit. I'm not talking about people writing to me; I'm just talking about in the spirit. It's hard for us to grasp God's normal, but God has already determined what He wants. His will is supposed to be our will. When we were saved, we were supposed to give up our will. But see, no one tells people that because the reaction is more like, "Well, I need a couple of days to think about that." You'll be drafted into an army that's at war, and you are not your own anymore. You have been bought with a price. But no one ever told me that.

So my body started acting up the next day after I was born again, and I started having all kinds of crazy thoughts. *Wait a minute. I'm saved, so what's going on here?* At that time, I didn't know that only one part of me was ruling and reigning, which was my spirit. My soul wasn't redeemed. But why are we not being taught this? After I realized only one part of me was redeemed and was ruling and reigning, I thought, *I've been robbed for years! Why hasn't anyone ever told me about this?*

We need to find out God's will, and we don't need to question it. God's will has always been displayed through Jesus Christ, and we never have to go back to God, asking Him for what we already know has been provided through the covenant. Jesus never made anyone sick or poor. Even in the Old Testament, God said, "There will be no poor among you; for the Lord will bless you in the land" (Deuteronomy 14:4 ESV). I already know it is God's will for me to be healed and to prosper. So it doesn't matter if I'm not healed instantly; I stand in faith, continuing to believe. When we understand these truths, we can then operate in them, and the enemy can no longer rob us because of what we don't know.

For us to help others, we must allow God to help us first. And we all need help. We need God to come into our finances and to come and heal our bodies. We need God to come and talk to our family members so they will encounter Him. Think about this; God wants to help us so that we can help others. We must remember it's not all about us. We know the gospel is good news to the poor and good news to the sick and those bound by the devil, and so we must share the good news with them so they can be delivered.

Your Case Is Closed

This truth is a major sticking point for most people. I want you to get this. When you start to encounter God's normal, you will then want to encounter His will. To do that, you must receive this revelation. "So now the case is closed. There remains no accusing voice of condemnation against those who are joined in life-union with Jesus" (Romans 8:1 TPT). Your case is closed! Did you know that this is the hardest truth for a Christian to step into? I'm not coming to you as a flight attendant who prays in tongues; right now, I'm coming to you as a prophet. And I'm telling you, by the Spirit of the Lord, if you get this truth, you will never be the same. You need to get over this: All the things you have done wrong do not exist in heaven anymore. I will hear about you and read about you in heaven because you will change history. Get over your past because, guess what? God already has, and it will never be mentioned again.

When I was in heaven, I was treated as though I had never sinned. Jesus talked to me as though I was one of His right-hand men. He told me, "You will rule and reign with me in eternity, forever, shoulder to shoulder, Kevin." How could this be? Because the case against me was closed, just as the case against you is closed! When I looked into Jesus's eyes, it wasn't as if He had never seen my file; it was as if it were gone. No record of it existed. I had the revelation that He didn't even know about my file because the Father chose to expunge it. Therefore, no judge could ever access it. You must know it is the same for you right now. I'm telling you, this is the main sticking point when encountering God's normal. There is no past sin when you are forgiven.

Please understand this; you're not just excused. It's as if it never happened. Do you hear me? Do not let any cloud without rain tell you otherwise. I'm done with false prophets and false ministers. When you preach the Word of God and God says you are forgiven, then you are forgiven. Period. I don't care if it's Greek, Hebrew, homebrew, or whatever. It's gone!

Now the devil will bring it up because he's the accuser of the brethren (Revelation 12:10). He's just doing his job, but remember, Jesus already made a fool of him when He disarmed principalities and powers, making a public spectacle of them, triumphing over them (Colossians 2:15). Don't you know that Jesus did that for us? Jesus didn't need to do that for Himself. He had already triumphed over the devil. The last time I checked, Jesus is on the throne, and satan got kicked out of heaven. Jesus even said, "I saw satan fall like lightning from heaven" (Luke 10:18). That's pretty fast. That was not just a kick out but a throw down. Come on, that's a smack down! That's crunching and crushing. I can hear those demons right now under my feet, mumbling. And I'm saying, "I can't hear you." Crunch, crunch.

When you get to heaven, you will not hear an accusing voice, and at that moment, you will realize you were robbed down here because you had false information about yourself. I don't want you to go through that because I already did. Jesus gave me a chance to do it right this time. And now, I really don't care what people think, but I do care about where they end up. It's actually all I care about. I'm sure your heart is in the same place as mine. I love people, and I want to help them. However, if they don't want my help, I will just focus on the people who do. I won't waste my time on religious people that are clouds without rain.

Walking in Freedom Is God's Normal

"Where the Spirit of the Lord is, there is freedom" (2 Corinthians 3:17). Wherever the Lord is, there is liberty, and since the Son has set you free, you are free indeed (John 8:36). The Spirit of the Lord is in you, and He is creating an atmosphere of freedom where you are walking with God, your Creator, and your Father. He loves you, and He has great plans for you.

When I was in heaven, I realized that everyone had this same spirit about them—liberty and freedom. The majority of the disciples were on the earth for a short time, and Jesus explained that they had killed some of the prophets and would kill Him too.

John the Baptist didn't last long either. He kept saying to Herod, "Hey, you can't have her as a wife" (Mark 6:18). The next thing you know, John lost his head. Many of you have encountered this kind of control in churches. It will sound something like, "You can't say this, and you can't do that." So when did it become about control?

I have said this before: Our government was formed to serve and protect us, not to tell us what to believe. The fivefold ministry was not established by God to control and manipulate you either. God's plan for the fivefold ministry is to perfect the body of Christ to the point where we are weaned off milk and onto eating meat. God intends for us to mature. We do not require being watched all the time.

God's Normal Is to Confront Religion

I want to address religion and those that do not preach the complete and authentic gospel. These people deny you access to the living God. When Jesus ripped the veil so that you could come in, He became your High Priest, and through Himself, He gave you the ability to become a king and a priest. You would want to know about becoming a king and a priest, right?

Now, if I wanted to control you, I would withhold that information from you. Why? Because religion keeps people poor, sick, and demonically oppressed. It always keeps them in a place of lack. The message is, "There is no deliverance, no healing, and no financial help from God anymore because all that died with the apostles." Religion will keep you from the benefits of God that we have obtained through Jesus Christ.

Jesus came and bought every good thing back for us. This is what Jesus said He came to fulfill: preach the good news to the poor, heal the sick, deliver people from their devils, seek and save those who were lost, and proclaim the year of Jubilee (Luke 4:19). What does this mean to us? Because of Jesus, I don't have to be sick, poor, and demonically oppressed. I now have eternal life, and I don't need to live with demon problems. I can be free from anything and everything. Now isn't that really good news?

"Religion can only cover sin. However, through Jesus, God entirely takes away all our sins."

When Jesus was on the earth fulfilling His ministry, He confronted the Pharisees because they were the religious system of the day. At one point, He addressed them, saying, "Brood of vipers! How can you, being evil, speak good things?" (Matthew 12:24). He confronted them and called them the sons of the devil (John 8:44).

After Adam and Eve ate the forbidden fruit, they grabbed what was nearest to them—fig leaves—to cover themselves. Jesus told me that is why He cursed the fig tree. They covered themselves with the fig leaves, which was their attempt to cover their sin. Religion can only cover sin; only through Jesus does God entirely take away all our sins, washing them, so there's no evidence left of your sin, period.

When Jesus was hungry and He came upon that fig tree, it had no fruit on it. So it had the form of a fig tree, but it denied the power of it. The fig tree represented the religion of Israel. So what did Jesus do? He hung Himself on a tree. "Christ has redeemed us from the curse of the law, having become a curse for us (for it is written, 'cursed is everyone who hangs on a tree')" (Galatians 3:13).

I really want you to take hold of this. Do not be deceived. A religion and a government will control the world. They will merge, and you can talk to those behind everything, those who have all the money and all the control. They don't want you here because you are hindering them and their agenda. The spirit that is in the religious system doesn't want you here either. This is why some religions kill Christians. If you study and learn from our forefathers during the Reformation, it will confirm that established religions have killed Christians. I won't allow the religious system to take me into their grasp, and neither should you. We know that our hope is in the resurrection, which has been deposited in us by the Holy Spirit, guaranteeing full payment.

God's Normal Brings Answers

When you discern that something is not right, do you get out of the water right away, or do you wait until it's boiling? Do you wait until the water reaches 110 degrees and remain there, wondering whether it will cool off? No, because you have the Spirit of power and you know and discern when a situation is not right. For instance, you may find yourself in a situation where you don't know what to do. You could be in a relationship or a difficult situation, whatever it may be, and you're seeking the Lord, asking for instruction. You're wondering, "What should I do?" Then, all of a sudden, the Spirit will quicken you and give you a word. This is why when I am preparing messages and speaking the Word of the Lord to people, I know that I need to be careful and stay sharp, being fully equipped with fire from the altar of God. And this must be true for you too. Because everything we do, whether we talk or we don't talk, should be fire.

God's Normal Is Overflow

Christians—not the devil's children—are supposed to manifest the favor of God. I'm serious. Think about it. Will we sit and argue, asking if God really wants to prosper us? I mean, are the devil's children allowed to prosper because that's just the way it is? Something has to change. Do you believe God at His Word, and do you trust Him? Is He a good Father? Yes, He is, and He wants to take care of you.

When you look at the old covenant, God's blessings for His children spoke to other nations with a message that demonstrated, "I am your God, and I'm going to prosper you. You'll be the head, not the tail. You'll do the lending, and you will not borrow" (Deuteronomy 28). Well, that sounds like overflow to me. God prospered Israel so that all the other nations would fear God, knowing He was prospering and moving powerfully on behalf of His children.

All the Old Testament stories carry this idea of not only knowing God and proclaiming Him as your God but that He rewards the trust that you have in Him with a demonstration of power so that everyone around you will see that you are favored.

Now Is the Time to Live in God's Normal

My prayer for you is that you will decide that now is the time to align yourself with God's normal and that you will walk in the revelation knowledge of what our heavenly Father has already given you. I can tell you that I've come to do His work, not my own, because I represent Him. He has asked me to defend Him to the people because He said that they were being slandered. My role is to tell people the good gospel and share that God is good.

CHAPTER 2

FAITH'S LADDER OF VIRTUES

So devote yourselves to lavishly supplementing your faith with goodness, and to goodness add understanding, and to understanding add the strength of self-control, and to self-control add patient endurance, and to patient endurance add godliness, and to godliness add mercy toward your brother and sisters, and to mercy towards others add unending love. Since these virtues are already planted deep within, and you possess the in abundant supply, they will keep you from being inactive or fruitless in your pursuit of knowing Jesus more intimately.

—2 Peter 1:5–8 TPT

These scriptures hold such a tremendous truth. I remember when I received the revelation on these verses. When I read, "So devote yourself to lavishly supplementing your faith," I used to think that faith was it. I mean, I went to a faith school. And you know what? When I graduated from that school, I thought that when Paul said, "three things remain: faith, hope, and love. But the greatest of these is love" (1 Corinthians 13:13), that the "greatest of these" was actually faith. I really did believe that. And I think many other people have gone to that same school and been taught the same. Here in 2 Peter, faith is the foundation but not the final destination that we are moving toward.

When I was in that school, I learned a lot about faith, but I didn't know my heavenly Father as I do now. I later came to know about the love of a heavenly Father. That's not the fault of the founder of the school but an example of an overemphasis on one aspect of the Bible so that there's no relationship. I don't remember the above passage being mentioned in the school, but see, Peter is saying here, "Faith is just the foundation. I want you to get that, and I want you to add these virtues to your faith."

Can you see that in our effort not to be religious, we actually become religious? Look at what it says. "Devote yourselves to supplement your faith with goodness and to your goodness add understanding, to your understanding add strength and self-control, and to your self-control add patient endurance and to endurance add godliness and to godliness add mercy and unending *love* toward your brothers, sisters and toward others" (emphasis added).

I really want you to understand this. You love God with all your heart, and you love your neighbor as yourself, so notice you can love yourself too. Just love your neighbor as well as you love yourself as people will then be healed because when Jesus healed the sick, His motivation was always compassion (Matthew 14:14; 20:34). This is key.

His compassion motivated Him.

Why? Because He loved the people to the point that He even loved the devil out of them.

Since we already have everything we need to live a godly life, we are without excuse. When you meet Jesus face-to-face, you won't be able to blame Him for anything. He has already done everything He needs to do, and now He's waiting for you. He's already made our enemies, His enemies, and they have become His footstool (Hebrews

10:13). He has already given us all the keys we need, and He's just waiting on us to apprehend.

Character Must Come First

Since these virtues are already planted deep within you and you possess them in an abundant supply, they will keep you. Notice it doesn't say that faith will keep you; it says, "these virtues will keep you." See how easily we can get off track? They will keep you from being inactive, which is good. But we must be fruitful in our pursuit of knowing Jesus Christ more intimately. We must decide.

As we continue, we get to where the rubber meets the road. This Scripture is saying, "to your faith, add all of these virtues." So faith is the starting point. I don't know about you, but I have not heard this message preached. This whole scenario has been completely left off the menu. And because of it, we do not have character. Yes, we talk about the gifts and we want to see miracles and we want to see the dead raised. But if you don't even show up for the funeral on time due to a lack of character, you can't raise someone from the dead. In other words, how can you pray and command someone to be raised from the dead if you don't even arrive?

But if anyone lacks these things, he is blind, constantly closing his eyes to the mysteries of our faith and forgetting his innocence, for his past sins have been washed away. For this reason, beloved ones, be eager to confirm and validate that God has invited you to salvation and claimed you as his own. If you do these things, you will never stumble. As a result, the kingdom's gates will open wide to you as God choreographs your triumphant entrance into the kingdom of our Lord and Savior, Jesus the Messiah. (2 Peter 1:9–11 TPT)

Open Your Eyes to the Mystery of Our Faith

Let's look at verse 9. "But if anyone is lacking these things, he is blind." One of the biggest problems that I see is people staying stationary. They keep their eyes closed, and they do not want God to move them on because of warfare. They feel as if they get hit every time they go forward, and God wants you to know that He is not the One doing all those things to you. It blows me away to even think about closing my eyes because I would miss something about the mysteries of God and the Holy Spirit.

At times, the Holy Spirit is taking me somewhere, and suddenly, I make a turn, and He's showing me something else. Then I'll think, *Whoa, I didn't see that coming*! I've been studying the Bible for a long time, but the Holy Spirit reveals new truth to me all the time. You must know that He wants to share all these intimate insights with you.

Peter continues by saying, "Forgetting his innocence because our past sins are washed away." If you don't know this, you will live your life forever as a victim. You will have a guilty conscience even though your conscience has already been cleansed. Just meditate on that for a moment: Even your conscience has been cleansed.

Verse 10 says, "For this reason, beloved ones, be eager to confirm and validate. That God has invited you to salvation and claimed you as his own." The Spirit of God wants to grab hold of you and walk you into confirmation and validation. You are supposed to be eager for that and let the Spirit of God lead you. God has invited you into this salvation, and He's claimed you as His own.

Just as the New Testament was written to Christians, these verses are too. Here, Peter wants us to understand that if you add all these virtues to your faith, you will not stumble. Think about that for a moment. You may have your certificate from the faith school you went to, but do you have your character certificate? Do you please God to the point where God takes you because He can't stand to be away from you? I mean, to the point that He wants to snatch you away as he did with Enoch (Genesis 5:24).

Peter wants you to know that after you have faith, if you lack adding these extra things, even after you receive your faith school certificate, you still must obtain your character certificate. Why is this so important? Because if you don't have your character certificate, you are blind, constantly closing your eyes to the mysteries of faith.

Religion Wants to Deny You Direct Access to God

This is a chronic issue today. People stay in the mindset of and living as victims, rooted in a religious and antichrist spirit. The spirit of religion keeps you out of the benefits of Christ, and the religious system does not want you to take action on your own. It is all set up to make you depend on another person so that you don't go directly to God yourself. What do you think a middleman is for?

That is why you must understand that God has established and made a way for you to add all these beautiful virtues to your faith. I believe that this is why Jesus sent me back: to preach and teach through Him, building onto what has already been established in the Word, and opening the revelation of the Scriptures to the body of Christ.

Fully Equipped and Ready at All Times

So I have a question for you. If you were saved permanently and could not lose your salvation, why would Peter say, "Be eager, beloved ones, to confirm and validate that God has invited you to salvation and He has claimed you as his own?" Why would he say that? He wants you to both confirm and validate this. Note these are two different words.

Let me give you an illustration. Do you remember Barney Fife? Barney had a uniform and a gun, but what if he only had one bullet available and kept it in his pocket and not in his gun? I mean, everything would seem fine until something went wrong, correct? If you remember *The Andy Griffith Show*, many shows were based on how Barney dealt with a situation.

So in comparison, when you're a Christian, dressed correctly, and wearing the uniform and the badge, you would think you would have everything you need. So I ask you, what does *everything* mean? It means nothing is left out. The problem occurs when you find yourself in a situation, and you don't know how to operate. But when the virtues are added to your faith, or in this example, to your uniform, you will be able to effectively handle every situation. At any given moment, you could say, "You know what? You have gone far enough. I'm arresting you."

It's Time to Wake Up

You must be aware that if you're not careful, religion (and the government) will strip you of the goodness of God and of His plans for your life. We can learn a lot about this just from observing God's creation. For example, Solomon wrote about the ant. When an anthill is kicked over, the ants immediately start rebuilding. They don't sit around and have a pity party about "these stupid humans who keep kicking over our cities." No, and they don't file lawsuits in court either. What do they do? They just start rebuilding right away. When their anthill gets kicked over, if you could hear them at night, they would be out there laughing, and in the morning, it's rebuilt again. And guess what? It's an even better version, new and improved. Why? It's in them because God created them that way. In other words, it's their character. It's time to wake up, church!

Peter says, "Beloved ones, be eager to confirm and validate that God has invited you to the salvation and that He claims you as his own." Right here, we realize it's all rigged in our favor. Some people think that's unscriptural, which is funny because this passage is right in 2 Peter 1:10. Jesus told me that it is rigged in our favor, and He showed me this verse, which validated what He said. If you add all these virtues to your faith, you will never stumble. You must realize that if you start letting man get in the way, it becomes false doctrine, and when this happens, the person who is being robbed is you.

If you were to believe the slant that the serpent gave Eve, you would fall into deception. Everything the serpent said was untrue and founded on lies, which is why Jesus said that satan is the father of lies. Just think, the devil could derail the whole human race by one conversation with someone who already had everything they needed. Why did Eve settle? Because she didn't know her relationship with the

Father. If she had known, why would she have ever questioned it? She forgot what God said or wasn't aware of it to begin with. Satan asked Eve, "Did God really say?" and then he said, "God knows that when you eat of it, you will be just like him" (Genesis 3:1–5). This is why we must know the whole counsel of God's Word.

Perter then says, "As a result of doing these things, the kingdom's gates will open wide to you as God choreographs your triumphant entrance into the eternal kingdom of our Lord and Savior, Jesus Christ" (2 Peter 1:11 TPT). This is such good news! You must know that you have everything that Jesus has, and you have Him too. As a result of this, you never have to worry. We must all fully embrace this truth. We will experience being co-glorified with Christ, provided that we accept His sufferings as our own.

> I won't hesitate to continually remind you of these truths, even though you are aware of them and are well established in the present measure of truth you have already embraced. And as long as I live, I will continue to awaken you with this reminder, since our Lord Jesus, the Anointed One, has clearly revealed that my departure is near (2 Peter 1:12–14 TPT)

Peter writes that he will continually remind them of these truths. Perhaps he thought, *I will keep telling them these things until I see these truths in action because I will know by the evidence of their fruit.* In other words, let's have some manifestation of faith. James said to show our faith by what we do (James 2:18). When he said that, he was talking about the manifestation of character.

When I worked for Southwest Airlines, I was awarded the President's Award, which is the highest honor you can receive. Other people I worked with had been there for years and had never received this award. I don't know how I got it, except the plaque made a note of my character. I explained that it was because I was a Christian. I thought I was just doing my job, but my performance was acknowledged as above normal, because I kept my word, showed up on time, was dependable, and loved and helped people. Just think, through God's precious promises, we can live like this every day.

Two Important Commands That We Live By

"Jesus said to him, 'You shall love the Lord your God with all your heart, with all your soul, and with all your mind.'

This is the first and great commandment. And the second is like it: 'You shall love your neighbor as yourself'" (Matthew 22:27–29). Keep in mind that Peter was well aware of his own human weakness. He was also aware that the church needed to be continually reminded and awakened to these truths because he knew his departure was drawing near. Jesus had a very similar conversation with the disciples when He said, "How long will I be with you?" (Matthew 17:17). He said this because of their lack of understanding.

"God knew we couldn't do any of this on our own, which is why He provided for us through these precious promises."

God knew we couldn't do any of this on our own, which is why He provided for us through these precious promises so that we can share in His divine nature, escaping the corruption that's in the world because of lust. It's the only way. Paul explained in Romans that under the law, man struggled. "For when we were in the flesh, the sinful passions which were aroused by the law were at work in our members to bear fruit to death. But now, we have been delivered from the law" (Romans 7:5–6). The fulfillment of the law is inside us now, and we obey these two commands: We love God with all our hearts, and we love our neighbors as ourselves.

Some people have difficulty believing that we can be part of the divine nature, but this is precisely what I saw in heaven. Just as it is written, "When they saw the boldness of Peter and John and perceived they were uneducated and untrained men, they marveled, and they realized these men had been with Jesus" (Acts 4:13). Just as people recognized that Peter and John had been with Jesus, they should recognize this about us.

Our Faith Is the Launching Pad

You must have a complete revelation and understanding of the point that Paul was making in 1 Corinthians 13 when he explained that you must have love and do all things in love because otherwise, it is just a clanging cymbal and you are nothing. Paul understood the truth and the necessity that we must be perfected in God's love.

Supplement your faith, add moral excellence and to moral excellence, add knowledge and to your knowledge, add self-control; and to self-control, add patient endurance and after patient endurance, add godliness and add brotherly affection. And with brotherly affection, add love for everyone. (2 Peter 1:5–7)

When I had given my life to the Lord, I thought I had been given an instant insurance policy. Later, in my Christian walk, I learned, "Congratulations, your life is not your own!" I was never told that in the beginning. Maybe some of you are in that same situation. I mean, do we really understand what we did when we gave our lives to the Lord? Is He entirely the Lord of our lives, or do we only have position? I pray that you would have both position and relationship.

This is important because I want to be perfected in the love of God and I want everything that I do to have value. Don't we all want that? None of us want to stand before the Lord and find out that we were just making a lot of noise and keeping busy, but in the end, none of it was fruitful.

At the beginning of this chapter, I told you that these verses in 2 Peter held such tremendous truths. So I want to ask you, are you ready for what's about to happen to you as you gain deeper revelation and add these virtues onto your faith? As we do this, Peter says that we will become more productive and useful in our knowledge of the Lord Jesus Christ (2 Peter 1:8 TPT). When I received a revelation of these verses, I realized that faith is the launching pad, so let's be sure we are adding all these wonderful virtues to our faith. "So, dear brothers and sisters, work hard to prove that you really are among those God has called and chosen. Do these things, and you will never fall away" (2 Peter 1:10 NLT).

Living Established in the Body

When Jesus walked me through the truths in 2 Peter, He also showed me that for the bride to be ready, we must work hard under grace to prove that we are among those who are called and chosen. The words "Work hard to prove you are really among those" jumped out at me, and I realized that I had thought I was secure all along.

Peter was a disciple, and he is explaining that we need to prove that we are really among those who were chosen and called. He then states, "And then you will never fail." This is exactly where I got the message, "It's Rigged in Your Favor." It's one of the best messages I have ever preached.

It came out of me because I saw that the environment of heaven wants to invade this earth, and that's favor, but the favor has to do with our participation and understanding that we must add these virtues and character traits to our faith. Second Peter 1:11 goes on to say, "Then God will give you a grand entrance into the eternal kingdom of our Lord and Savior, Jesus Christ."

We must realize two ways that people will try to come against these truths. They will try to compromise the message itself, or they will try to remove the messenger. If you do not compromise these truths, others will try to come against you as they did with Jesus. They tried to silence Him until He chose to go to the cross.

When Lazarus had died, Jesus didn't arrive on the scene until he had been dead for four days. Jewish custom teaches that a person's spirit stays with them up to the third day, and after that, it departs to Paradise. Jesus purposely waited to arrive on the fourth day, which is why the ladies were screaming and so mad at him.

After Jesus raised Lazarus from the dead, the news spread to such a large crowd among the Jewish people that many more people believed in Jesus, so the Pharisees plotted to kill Lazarus (John 12:9–11). They wanted to shut him up so he couldn't tell others what Jesus had done for him. They knew what a living, walking, talking testimony of Jesus's miracles would do.

You must understand, regardless of whether you hide in a cave or stand on your street and preach, people will try and get you to compromise and tone it down, or they will just want to take you out. We already know that satan wants to take us out, but he can't, and you have to determine, "I will do what God wants me to do, and no one can take me out until it's my time." We just need to ensure that our hearts are turned toward God. If you are reading this book and your heart is turned away from God, turn your heart and your face back to Him right now. Place your complete focus back on Jesus, and don't allow satan to distract you or discredit Jesus because of different things that have happened to you.

Come Out and Be Separate

We have the same protection from God that the Israelites had when the death angel passed over their homes (Exodus 12). They had the blood on their doorposts, but we have a better covenant because His blood *completely* covers us. When God told Moses to tell the Israelites to borrow gold and silver from their neighbors, essentially taking all their jewelry, they started to become their own nation as the nation of the people of God (Exodus 3). Since Egypt represents the world, this was a picture of their separation from the world by leaving and going out. This is how we are to live, coming out from among unbelievers and separating ourselves from them (2 Corinthians 6:17).

I will not live nervously or flinch. No! I cannot be bought, coerced, manipulated, or controlled, and neither can you. We have been set free, and we are free indeed. Now is the time to bind up, loose, and get an attitude. When we live as free people, we begin having spiritual revelation encounters, which demonstrates that the Word of God is at work in our lives. When the Word of God starts manifesting, you become like one of those excessive people. Now someone may argue, "Some people have faith; others have good deeds." But I say, "How can you show me your faith if you don't have good deeds? I will show you my faith by my good deeds" (James 2:18 NLT).

James is explaining that his deeds manifest the reality of his faith. This is the difference between a person that calls themselves a Christian but denies the power of God and someone who truly is among those who God has called and chosen. As I have said before, religious people are clouds without rain. Paul said not to even eat with them. Religious people are in bondage, they are broke, they can't get over their addictions, and they have no power in their lives. They will criticize you for walking in the power of God, and the challenge is that they don't see that they're in bondage.

Jesus said, "Whoever commits sin is a slave to sin" (John 8:34). He was going for the jugular, the sin problem. He was going after the religious people. Religious people do not know that they have been forgiven of their sins because they have not believed in Jesus. True believers could never live any differently because we walk in the power of God. The blood of Jesus was enough to put us over, and we demonstrate God's glory to the point that everyone wants it—they want what you have. According to Romans 11:14, we are supposed to be provoking people to jealousy in hopes of saving some of them. We are to support the gospel and come alongside those that are doing the same. We are to help an orphan or a widow or those who cannot help themselves.

The Benefits of God's Normal

"Jesus answered them, 'Most assuredly, I say to you, whoever commits sin is a slave of sin. And a slave does not abide in the house forever, but a son abides forever. Therefore if the Son makes you free, you shall be free indeed'" (John 8:34–36). When Jesus said, "a son abides forever," he was talking about the privileges, about all the benefits that we have as sons of God. Sometimes a job opportunity will have such great benefits that people will desire the benefits even more than the income they will be receiving.

That is how it was for me. My benefits were very nice when I worked for Southwest Airlines. The stock was split, which meant they issued more shares to shareholders without diluting the value of their stakes every year, and it didn't matter how much you were making an hour; you received this benefit. To me, it was the fact that I was a part of something that was exploding, and for thirty years, I watched the company prosper. As born-again believers, we need to give the Word of God first place in our lives because that is where the true benefits package is because we know the Word of God is incorruptible.

> *"When you ask God for vision, then you speak out what you are seeing from your Father. This is where the division starts happening."*

The Separation of the Sheep from the Goats

The separation of the sheep from the goats is happening in the body right now. Jesus knew that the Word of God wasn't in the Pharisee's hearts because He said, "I know that you are Abraham's descendants, but you seek to kill Me because My word has no place in you" (John 8:37). Jesus was saying that having Abraham as their father was not enough because one greater than Abraham was standing before them. In verse 39, Jesus continues, "If you were Abraham's children, then you would be doing the works of Abraham." So Jesus was attributing the benefits of being the children of Abraham with action, which was a manifestation of the evidence that their faith was not real. Then Jesus took it a step further and said, "You are of your father the devil, and the desires of your Father you want to do. He was a murderer from the beginning, and does not stand in the truth, because there is no truth in him" (John 8:44).

God's Spirit Moving through You

I think we have established that faith without works is dead, right? But to clarify, the works you are doing are not because you have to earn your salvation; we do not need to do that. Jesus has already taken care of that for us. However, what it does look like is allowing the Spirit of God in you to start healing people around you, prophesying people's futures to them, and speaking their good and expected end instead of pronouncing judgment on people or adding burdens to them, which is why Jesus confronted the Pharisees.

A New Testament prophet does not pronounce judgment. When the disciples asked if they should call down fire upon a city, Jesus rebuked them and said, "You do not know what manner of spirit you are of" (Luke 9:55). Do not be like Jonah and get mad when a city or a people repents because that means they are turning back to God. Do not get mad at me for saying this—Jesus said it, John the Baptist said it, and every prophet said it. If you are doing this, you need to repent because it is wrong.

We need to repent for our nation and repent personally for our unbelief and lukewarmness. It has always been about repentance, humility, the cross, and living the crucified life. This is not a new doctrine. It just needs to be brought to the forefront again. When we hear God's words, we obey them because there's only one way—Jesus—and there is no other way. There's no shortcut or button to speed up the process. Listen, God loves us, but He wants us to be His children, which means He wants to manifest His benefits through us so that people will know by our works that we are His child.

This Is Not a Test

How many times have you spoken to someone about the Word of God, and they weren't able to discern your words? When this happens, it is because a person must be spiritually discerned to understand the Word. I say this because I am wondering when you will get over people criticizing and coming against you? When will you just walk away from those kinds of relationships?

See, the separation has come. I'm giving you a heads up; it's already happened! We are the body, and we are to stand out from among them and "be ye separate," and some people will lose out. This is not a test; it's the real deal. But we will pass the test, and we will be in Goshen as we will not be part of the coming judgment. We are protected because we are

His children, and the Bible says that we are not appointed to wrath (1 Thessalonians 5:9). It doesn't matter what a person believes about the rapture—pre-, mid-, or post-Tribulation—we have not been appointed to God's wrath, and that is the truth.

Jesus, the Preexistent Christ

In John 8:48, the Jews said to Jesus, "Do we not say rightly that you are a Samaritan and have a demon?" Wow, this is worse than calling Him the son of fornication. Do you want to know why? Samaritans were considered half-breeds. So here, we see that they have thrown a racial attack at Him. They called Him a Samaritan, but He was pure stock Jewish. They called Him that because they did not know who His Father was. They automatically believed that whoever He was, He wasn't a Jew.

They were going after His origin because satan knew that the only way he could ever defeat Jesus would be to attack His identity. When Jesus was in the desert, satan said, "*If* you are the Son of God, turn this rock into bread." Jesus was probably thinking, *Whatever, devil, you know who I am. I made you.* But see, Jesus came as the Son of Man. He was already the Son of God, but He didn't defend Himself; His Father would do that for Him.

You cannot mess with a preexistent Christ because you can't mess with the foundation of the universe; it's the very foundation of the throne. Jesus said, "So my Father, restore me back to the glory that we shared together when we were face-to-face before the universe was created" (John 17:4–5 TPT). I want you to know that this is God's normal. Jesus was preexistent. His Father was God; did we forget that? Do we have to wait until "O Little Town of Bethlehem" starts playing on the radio at Christmas to remember that He was pre-existent and that Mary was a virgin?

So religious people will go after the origin of your faith. They cannot handle a God who rigged it in your favor before you were born and set it up so that you can do this life and do it so that they'll remember you forever where you will be noted in history. Are you seeing the opportunity that you have here as His children? Do you see how satan uses the religious system to undermine your origin? You are a child of God!

Living from the Manifestation of Our Faith

We live from the manifestation of our faith when we answer questions about why people are here or make them aware of what they are missing when they don't even know they are missing anything. We let them know how to live an abundant life in Christ. Why can we do this? Because we have the answers people need. You are an ambassador; you are the sons and daughters of God, so you have the answers. They will know you by your fruit (Matthew 7). Religion will try to get you to do the actions without life and abundant experience. They will shut you down if you start to have an experience.

How did Jesus respond to their attempted racial accusation? He said, "I do not have a demon; but I honor My Father, and you dishonor Me. And I do not seek My own glory; there is One who seeks and judges" (John 8:49–50). Do you notice that Jesus didn't defend Himself? Instead, in verse 51, He says, "Most assuredly, I say to you, if anyone keeps My word he shall never see death." This seriously got to them because the Jews went on to say, "Now we know that You have a demon! Abraham is dead, and the prophets; and You say, 'If anyone keeps My word he shall never taste death.' Are You greater than our Father Abraham, who is dead? And the prophets are dead. Who do you make Yourself out to be?" (John 8:52–53). Jesus was like, "I'm glad you asked." He replied,

> "If I honor myself, my honor is nothing. It is my Father who honors Me, of whom you say that He is your God. Yet you have not known Him, but I know Him. And if I say, 'I do not know Him,' I shall be a liar like you; but I do know Him and keep His word. Your father Abraham rejoiced to see My day, and he saw it and was glad." Then the Jews said to him, "You are not yet fifty years old, and have You seen Abraham?" Jesus said to them, "Most assuredly, I say to you, before Abraham was, I AM." (John 8:54–58)

Mic drop on verse 58! Again, Jesus is saying, "I am the pre-existent Christ." The Pharisees then took up stones to throw at Him, and Jesus hid and went out of the temple, going through the midst of them (John 8:59). Notice that the stones were in the temple. These were the stones that they used to pass judgment on people.

What you just read is prophetic in every single way. It would be the same as if I lined you up and gave you a prophetic word. This is religion, which still exists. We must find a place where we can walk in our sonship and in the demonstration of power—a place where we can freely worship. We know who Jesus is, and so we can be confident that He will not hide from us because we accept that before Abraham was, He was.

Paul explained in 2 Corinthians 5:16, "Therefore, from now on, we regard no one according to the flesh. Even though we have known Christ according to the flesh, yet now we know Him thus no longer." Just as it says in 1 Corinthians, these truths were once hidden. They are from ages past, and now the Spirit is revealing those deep hidden things of God to us (1 Corinthians 2:10). The same glory that God shared with the Son, He's sharing with us now, and we are one with God.

The Word of God Ignites Our Spirits

I have determined that I won't listen to people who are in unbelief because I know what will happen if I do. I do not want what happened to the children of Israel to happen to me.

As has just been said: 'Today, if you hear his voice, do not harden your hearts as you did in the rebellion.' Who were they who heard and rebelled? Were they not all those Moses led out of Egypt? And with whom was he angry for forty years? Was it not with those who sinned, whose bodies fell in the desert? And to whom did God swear that they would never enter his rest if not to those who disobeyed? So, we see that they were not able to enter because of their unbelief. (Hebrews 3:15–19 NIV)

Because of their unbelief, they did not enter into the promises. Now, we are accountable. All the stories in the Old Testament were types and shadows of that which was to come. All of it is for good instruction, reproof, and doctrine. The New Testament was formed out of manifestation by the Holy Spirit. The Spirit of God moved upon people, and they wrote the Word of God. That is why when we hear the Word, it ignites our spirits because they came from God's Spirit. This is why we must not allow a religious devil to talk us out of what's coming next, which is manifestation. Praise God, as I write this, I can feel the powers of the coming age!

Established in Christ

"And because of his glory and excellence, he has given us great and precious promises. These are the promises that enable you to share his divine nature and escape the world's corruption caused by human desires" (2 Peter 1:4). We have established that we have everything we need to live a godly life (2 Peter 1:3). That means we are without excuse. When you meet Jesus face-to-face, you won't be able to blame Him for anything. He has done everything He's going to do. Now He's waiting for you. He has already made all His enemies His footstool through the churches, and He's given us the keys. He is waiting for us to "cast down arguments and every high thing that exalts itself against the knowledge of God, bringing every thought into captivity (apprehend and arrest) to the obedience of Christ" (2 Corinthians 10:5, words in parentheses are the author's).

CHAPTER 3

Undone in the Presence of God

In the year that King Uzziah died, I saw the Lord sitting on a throne high and lifted up, and the train of His robe filled the temple. Above it stood seraphim; each one had six wings; with two he covered his face, with two he covered his feet, and with two he flew. And one cried to another and said: "Holy, holy, holy is the Lord of hosts; the whole earth is full of His glory!" And the posts of the door were shaken by the voice of him who cried out, and the house was filled with smoke.

So I said: "Woe is me, for I am undone! Because I am a man of unclean lips, and I dwell in the midst of a people of unclean lips; For my eyes have seen the King, the Lord of Hosts."

—Isaiah 6:1–5

NORMAL

When Isaiah encountered the holiness and the glory of God, he immediately cried out, "Woe is me, for I am undone!" This is what happens when you encounter God's normal. At times, it will seem difficult to adjust. Everything was fine for Isaiah as he was going about the Lord's business on earth. Then, in a moment, he was in heaven, encountering God and seeing the activity around the throne. Isaiah was a major prophet called to Israel, yet in Isaiah 6, when he writes about the holiness and the glory of God that he encountered in the throne room, he was undone and saw himself as unclean. He says, "I am a man of unclean lips, and I live among people of unclean lips." I have talked about how important our words are many times because this is what Jesus said to me. So what would make your words unclean? Speaking the wrong words.

It will be the same with you; one moment, you'll be going about your life thinking everything is just fine, and then the next moment, you will have an encounter with God. Suddenly, it's not fine anymore because you haven't been accustomed to God's normal. When we are touched by the almighty God within His presence, we are forever changed. He changes everything; He makes it better. Here in this realm, you're going through a terrible time, because in this fallen world, you're being tested through the world system, which we know does not treat us fairly. Additionally, you are being persecuted because you are a child of God. When you encounter God's glory and holiness, it's so far away from what you know, and you become completely undone, which is a positive thing.

> Then one of the seraphim flew to me, having in his hand a live coal which he had taken with the tongs from the altar. And he touched my mouth with it, and said: "Behold, this has touched your lips; Your iniquity is taken away, And your sin purged." Also I heard the voice of the Lord, saying: "Whom shall I send, And who will go for Us?" Then I said, "Here am I! Send me." (Isaiah 6:6–8)

When Isaiah encountered God, it was way too much for him. The only solution was for an angel to introduce a coal from God's altar onto his lips, cleansing his lips. He then responded in complete surrender, saying, "Lord, I'll be your messenger." After his encounter with God's normal, he went back and finished his calling as a prophet, writing an amazing sixty-six chapters that included the prophecies of the Messiah.

I say all the time that you need to be ready for this to happen. So many people have told me that they want a visitation from Jesus and an angel. My response to them is always, "Are you ready for a change?" I'm telling you, it will change you, and you will reach a place where you don't want these experiences to happen as often as you think because you will have to make a lot of decisions and become accountable. I honestly don't know how people function the way they do. There really must be more accountability in the body of Christ.

If you have already been to heaven, well, congratulations. But I want to know how you are. Because you will change. Do you have angelic visitations every week? Well then, I want to know what God is doing through you because angels aren't coming to play cards. What I'm trying to show you here is how all this has turned into a carnival. God is not our entertainment. God is to be known; He's to be known in His ways, not known by His acts. Israel knew God's acts, but Moses knew His ways (Psalm 103:7). You get to know His ways by changing your diet, getting off milk, and eating the meat of the Word.

The Time for Accountability Is Now

People are so hungry for an encounter with God that will result in the outpouring of God's Spirit. I have seen the future and what the upcoming outpouring will look like. I don't think anyone realizes the fullness of God's power that is about to be poured out. People will be lying out in church services everywhere. You will hear how people are being healed and how they will experience amazing, supernatural events, and everyone will know that the miracles are coming from a move of God's Spirit.

For this to come into the fullness that God is planning, people must become accountable. You will have to be willing to walk under the anointing if you want the anointing. You will have to walk in the revelation if you want the revelation. We must understand the importance of accountability and how it relates to the outpouring of the Spirit. We must also consider what will happen if God decides to move in and does not leave. What will it look like when this move becomes a habitation?

I've been to the future, and I've seen everyone in the throne room worshipping the Lamb, and everything is fine. I can tell you that we're all going to make it. I know in our lives down here, we're trying to figure out just how we'll get through each day, but God has already received us and we make it. However, I want to be very serious with you right now. The time for accountability is now. We must learn how to walk in the spiritual things that we have been asking God for, the things we have been wanting and desiring.

"Let His normal cause you to become undone so that you say, 'Yes, Lord, I will be your ambassador.'"

It's Time to Check Our Hearts

The Spirit of the Lord has told me to tell the body to stop being critical. Stop judging people and just focus on Jesus. We are to walk in forgiveness and in love toward everyone. Encounter God's normal and allow it to shift you. Let His normal cause you to become undone so that you say, "Yes, Lord, I will be your ambassador. Just send me back, and I'll be your messenger." If you do that, you will have plenty of encounters because you will have turned your focus from inward to outward. You no longer focus on yourself, only caught up with what pertains to you. Instead, you will minister to others, and then God will minister to you.

You must flip it on the devil. The devil is trying to trap you into thinking you're victimized. You then expect the next bad thing to happen at any moment. Once you start living and doing things for others, loving them with His love, nothing will happen the way you normally expect it to. You'll think, *Something has changed. Nothing bad happened to me today.* And then each day, you think the same thing with the same result. You realize you might have a trend here. You think, *Maybe the gospel is having an effect on me so that I only have good news on my lips and only good things happening in my life.*

This is how you start experiencing the favor of God, and the devil stops tripping you up. Here, you begin to have power over your will and your flesh. You will have the power to break addictions. If you are willing to walk in love toward one another and become accountable for what God has given you, you can walk in the miracle power of God in these last days. Why? Because that's God's normal, and from here, you can walk in complete fulfillment of God's will for your life.

We Bless Others from Our Blessings

Did you know it is God's normal that you not only walk in His perfect will but that you also walk out of poverty and never go back? Yes, you could be debt free because it is God's normal. For some people, this is entirely new because they are hearing it for the first time. God never wanted you to be in debt, not even under Old Testament law. Part of the blessing for the children of Israel was no debt, which showed other nations that God was with them. He said you would lend, but you will never borrow money (Deuteronomy 15:6). So how did we get into this situation?

I found out that the word "mortgage" is made up of two words: *mort* and *gage* which actually means "death grip."[1] The day I discovered this, I told Kathi, "This isn't good," and from that moment on, we believed that God would help us pay off our mortgage. We have continued helping other people pay off their debts, helping them relieve the financial

---

[1] Libby Kane, "The origins of the word 'mortgage' will make you think twice about buying a house," *Business Insider*, March 16, 2016, https://www.businessinsider.com/mortgage-means-death-pledge-2016-3. "mortgage (n.)" accessed September 17, 2021, https://www.etymonline.com/word/mortgage.

burden. We even helped people pay their mortgages, and because of that, God paid our mortgage in full.

And now we are free of that bondage. God wants to set more people free. This is what will happen; you will encounter your heavenly Father, and He will shift your perspective. When He shifts your perspective, you won't want to live like you do now. You will want to live in a place where all of God's heart as your loving heavenly Father is fulfilled for you.

God wants you to usher in the second coming of Christ, and He wants you to provide for others after He has blessed you. He wants you to lay hands on the sick. He wants you to cast out devils. First, you get rid of the devils in your life, and then you help others. You start a Bible study; you begin to write. You begin to sing, and you start to play instruments; you do whatever the Spirit of God is telling you to do.

And yes, you can teach the Bible. I mean, you can read the Bible and study it, right? Then you can teach it. At Warrior Notes, we will train people to lead Bible studies and start home fellowships. We will teach people how to pray and how to lay hands on the sick so that they will recover. The

Lord has shown me how to help in every area of people's lives because I want us to wrap it up down here. The body of Christ must be built up, not torn down. Many ministries are addressing current events in our world, but that is not what the Spirit of the Lord is saying to me, so I'm following my heavenly Father's will. Whatever the Father is doing, that's what I will do, and whatever He is saying, that's what I will say.

The Abundant Life in Christ

By Jesus Christ's stripes, we are healed; that is in the Old and New Testament. This truth has never changed; God doesn't have any sickness to give you. I don't care what you were taught before; the devil is giving people sickness and then making it look like God is doing it. Nothing has changed when it comes to the devil; it's the same old thing, and we have his playbook. We already know what he will do before he does it. The devil will kill, steal, and destroy, but Jesus came to give us life and life more abundantly (John 10:10).

So what will I do? I will talk about life and life more abundantly. I will use the word "abundantly" all the time until the people that don't like that word just go away. If you don't want abundant life, then you can't accept Jesus Christ. Jesus *is* abundant life. He is giving us life and life more abundantly. Not only is He giving this to us, but He's also giving it to us in such a gracious measure that it's exceedingly above and beyond what we could ever think or imagine (Ephesians 3:20). He truly is such a good, kind, heavenly Father.

When Isaiah encountered God's normal, he changed to the point that it not only affected him but affected his entire generation and all future generations because the book of Isaiah is still being read today. Because of his encounter with God, he become one of the greatest prophets that ever lived. It was the same for King David. God's normal became his normal, and then he killed giants. David went on to become king, and out of his lineage came the Messiah. According to Psalm 89, David would be in a covenant with God forever. David encountered God's normal, and supernatural events happened in his life. I want you to understand that this is God's normal for you, too, because this is what God has called you to. It is His plan for your life.

Never doubt what God is doing in you and for you, even if you think you haven't seen it fully manifest yet. You've had an amazing seed sown into you, and that seed is forever. I know I will see a harvest on the seed I'm sowing for eternity. It will never end. We will all see a harvest when we sow the Word of God.

> *"I am telling you, the Word of God transforms people's lives so that they will never be the same."*

If you have found yourself fighting with God about receiving His normal in your life, you can adjust your heart right now. Whatever it is, just agree with Him that you'll finish your race the right way, focusing on the gospel message, lifting up Jesus, yielding yourself in a place of humility before God, and doing whatever He is calling you to do. When you come into agreement with His plan, He will lift you up in due season; the plans that God has in store for you will happen. But you will go through a process, and the time will come when you will see the fruit. It will manifest because of the incorruptible Word of God that has been sown in you. I am telling you, the Word of God transforms people's lives so that they will never be the same.

I am so thankful that the Lord showed me the future. I saw the results of my faithfulness and how people's lives were forever changed as I preached the gospel message and lifted up Jesus. I saw we had to go through a time and a season of testing, but the people of God rose to the occasion so that they locked into the track that God had called them to. And I'm telling you this because you're included too.

At the airlines, I worked up to thirteen hours a day to retire early. At the time, I had all kinds of physical issues and challenges. I was having problems with my sinuses and ears to the point that it became unbearable to fly, but I had to fly every day. I continued and finished working until retirement.

Let us agree together that we will stay right in there with God. Commit in your heart right now that no matter what you are going through, you're going on with Him. When you make this heart commitment, I can guarantee that you will look back and see that God was faithful. You will be able to see that He had a plan and that the Word of God does not fail because it will produce a crop in you.

Sitting on a Throne in Heaven

"To him who overcomes I will grant to sit with Me on My throne, as I also overcame and sat down with My Father on

His throne" (Revelation 3:21). When I was in heaven, I got to sit on the throne mentioned in Revelations 3:21, which was very uncomfortable for me at first because of my religious thinking, even though I knew better. I was beside myself at the sight of the myriads of angels and saints as far as I could see, worshipping the Lamb who was seated beside me. I never saw His face, but I knew the Father was a very young man, and I had a knowing that He hadn't aged a bit. At the same time, I knew He was the Ancient of Days. At that moment, I saw all the Scriptures, and I knew that this was God's normal, the way that He operates.

I ask, what is it that you need from the Lord right now, because God meets all your needs according to His riches in glory? The parallel realm in heaven is perfect. However, a disconnect seems to exist between the heavenly and earthly realms. People are feeling abandoned, lonely, and forgotten, but you are not! God is present with you right now, and when God said that He would never leave you or forsake you, He meant it. There is never a disconnect, and our time and delays do not affect God. When you pray or even think of a need, God already knew it before you even asked. He already had the answer, and He released it the moment you prayed (Matthew 6:8).

The Power of Jesus's Authority

As I sat beside Jesus, I experienced just how much authority He has, and yet I could stand with Him if He allowed me to. It required Him to give me strength to stand there. He would tell me, "We're going to go here, and we're going to do this, and I want to show you something." He would then hold His hand up, and the destination knew it had to come to us. Whatever the destination He had commanded just enveloped us. We were going from place to place, but we never went anywhere. I encountered God's normal, and He told me to write about what I saw. He wants His children to know so that they can have understanding and revelation about His normal. It can then become their normal too.

During this time with Jesus, He showed me things about this earth realm and the Spirit realm and that we can win down here because of all He accomplished. When you came to Him and He saved you, He did not automatically rapture you because if that is all it was about, Jesus would have taken you with Him then. God has another plan for us. So we have no need to stay in a bomb shelter with our beans and rice for the rest of our lives, watching DVDs about the dragon, the seventh seal, and the third bowl of wrath. Unfortunately, many people have this mentality and are deceived, but that's not what it's about. During our time here, we let the Holy Spirit speak to us and move us in demonstration power to show the unsaved who Jesus is. We love our family, friends, and anyone we can because we know we have the good news and that we are His ambassadors.

No Vacancy Here

People have told me that you cannot address the devil. Well, Jesus already has, and He told us to do the same. My thought is that there is a devil. He gets driven out, and I don't let him rest; it's pretty straightforward to me. I don't even let him set up his little pup tent. Jesus gave us a hint when He told us that when a spirit leaves a person, it goes into arid places, and then it will try to come back (Matthew 12:43). We do not let them back in. When a demon leaves you, it goes out, trying to find a better place, someone who is weaker and won't fight back. However, if the demon can't find a person, he knows where you are, so he tries to come back. When he does, he finds out you have now been entirely filled with the Spirit and have now taken the stance that you are no longer a victim.

The enemy then finds out that there is no more vacancy. Move along, no vacancy here. You have now outgrown your invisible friend because you have nothing in common with him anymore. You don't need his addictions, and as a matter of fact, you don't need anything from him or about him. The truth is, if you haven't given the enemy domain to be there, you just drive him out.

God finally released me to share what I had seen when I went to heaven so that I could help people connect the dots. I waited twenty-three years to release my first book, and it wasn't about the money; it was personal. I know I had always wanted someone to do that for me, but I couldn't find anyone. I wanted to help people by giving them a peek, giving them strategies, at what's going on in the spirit realm. I have learned to beat the devil in every game he plays so that he just gives up. You finally reach the point where you're not cooperating with them, and they'll just go on to someone weaker.

What We See from the Second Realm Is Conditional

"He is the image of the invisible God, the firstborn over all creation. For by Him, all things were created that are in heaven and that are on earth, visible and invisible, whether thrones or dominions or principalities or powers. All things were created through Him and for Him" (Colossians 1:15–16). In the Bible, we have examples of prophets seeing into all the realms, including the second heaven, which is the realm where evil spirits are. We need to know that when God shows us events, they do not necessarily have to happen that way. God gives us warnings and shows us the future, and He can provide us with strategies through dreams and visions.

So our immediate response should be, "Okay, Lord, I see what you're showing me. We can change that. What do you want to do?" Now prophets can get it wrong when they only speak what they see in the second heaven and don't ask or seek God to find out His plan. We must remember that what we see from that realm is conditional.

For example, He might show you the enemy's plans about a situation like when He showed me the future destruction of locations, including burning cities. Still, when He reveals these events, you now have this inside information, and you have authority, so you can pray as He tells you to. What if you're not entirely sure that you have this authority? Well, Jesus made it clear when He said, "Assuredly, I say to you, whatever you bind on earth will be bound in heaven, and whatever you loose on earth will be loosed in heaven" (Matthew 18:18). He's just waiting for us to agree with Him. Now this is like faith on steroids for most people. When you were born again of the Spirit, you became a son or a daughter of the living God, and you are to speak God's will.

A great example of someone who knew his authority and knew that what came from the second realm was conditional was an intercessor named Rees Howells. God used him to change nations and history, and you know what? We can do the same. God will show us what satan is planning and how to stop him in his tracks. We have the Word, and we also pray in the Spirit.

Prophecy Is Conditional

We are part of the new covenant, which means we live by faith. "Faith in what?" you may ask. Faith in God's Word! This is why Paul told Timothy to wage war with the prophecies he had received. See, you have to actively wage war with the prophetic words spoken to you and beat the living daylights out the devil with them. You must make the connection between what is already the truth in heaven and bring it here to this realm.

So, leaders, I ask you to coach prophets and prophetesses, making sure that they know that prophecy is conditional based on the fact that Jesus Himself was limited in His own hometown because of unbelief. If we focus too much on end times, it will happen. However, it's not supposed to happen yet, and we don't want the antichrist to sit on his throne in this generation, do we? No, we want the antichrist to die unseated, and that includes all the ones that we think might even be living on the earth today. "Then Jesus said to them again, 'I am going away, and you will seek Me, and will die in your sin. Where I go, you cannot come'" (John 8:21).

God's Normal in Prayer

The mysteries of God and the movement of the Spirit are deep, and they manifest through your mouth, through your life, and through your beliefs. It becomes who you are. The church should be the most powerful institution on the earth since we've been given the keys and the authority to bind and loose in this realm. Here in John, Jesus was talking to the Pharisees, the goats, and the religious people that claim to know God but deny the power of the resurrection. He tells them, "Where I go, you cannot come because you are from beneath and I am from above." Uh-oh. Separation is coming.

Now, this is the point I want to make regarding how we pray from the realm of heaven. I want to share the key with you. In John 8:26, Jesus said, "He who has sent me is true, and I speak to the world those things which I heard from Him." Jesus doesn't go beyond what He's seen God doing or what He's heard from God, even though He knows a whole lot more. In the same way, He knows a whole lot more about you and what He has for you and what He wants to do. All of it is so amazing, and He's so excited for you.

In John 8:28–29, Jesus goes on to say, "When you lift up the son of man, then you will know that I am He, and that I do nothing of Myself; but as My Father has taught me, I speak these things. And He who sent Me is with Me. The Father has not left Me alone, for I always do those things that please Him." This Scripture holds a key to prayer; He only did those things that pleased His Father. "Then Jesus said to those Jews who believed Him, 'If you abide in My word, you are my disciples indeed. And you shall know the truth, and the truth shall set you free'" (John 8:31–32). Jesus is saying that when we are abiding in the Word, which is Jesus, and our hearts are to please the Father, we then add receiving the truth and begin encountering God's normal in prayer. You are encountering the truth directly from the Father. We also know we have the Spirit of truth, who is our Counselor, living in us, and He leads us into all truth.

"But God, who is rich in mercy, because of His great love with which He loved us, even when we were dead in trespasses, made us alive together with Christ and raised us up together, and made us sit together in the heavenly places in Christ Jesus" (Ephesians 2:3–5). What ever happened to us ruling and reigning in Christ? We have been raised up together with Christ, and God made us to sit together in the heavenly places in Christ Jesus, right? This is God's plan; we were made to rule and reign on this earth through our authority in Christ.

The Spirit of God can come into each one of us as we yield to Him. We take prophecy and wage war with it so that it is no longer conditional; it becomes absolute truth if we believe it. We can take what God has shown us from the second realm as we see the plan and strategy of satan, knowing that it is conditional and that we have the key and the authority to change the outcome.

CHAPTER 4

On Earth as it is in Heaven

The disciples said to Jesus, Lord, teach us to pray.
So, Jesus taught them this prayer: "Our heavenly
Father, may the glory of your name be the center on
which life turns. May your Holy Spirit Come upon
us and cleanse us. Manifest your kingdom on
earth."
—Luke 11:1-2 TPT

When Jesus walked here among us, He demonstrated what it looked like to transfer the reality of heaven to earth. We must realize that Jesus continuously operated in God's normal. Within this reality, as disciples of Christ, we too walk in God's normal. As His disciples, we adhere to what our Master is saying and doing just as Jesus did. Jesus demonstrated an impartation to the disciples as He showed them heaven's reality from the Father. Through this impartation, the disciples heard their Master's word; they mixed it with their faith so that it took hold and manifested in their hearts.

It is the same for you now as a disciple of Jesus. When you have ears to hear, you will adhere to God's Word so that replication manifests in your life. As this occurs, you begin to look like Jesus so that people notice that you have been with Him just as they noticed that Peter and John had been with Him (Acts 4:13). So I ask you this, didn't the disciples turn the world upside down? How did this happen? You see, it's a domino effect. And this is what I want to do as my part here on the earth. I want to see Jesus replicated, and I want the power of God to be given back to believers instead of just to the fivefold ministry.

Remember that our heavenly Father initiates everything, and He has made everything; even the worlds were made through Him (Hebrews 1:2). As believers, we know our Father's voice, and we receive the impartation and the manifestation through the Word. When Jesus speaks and the Holy Spirit ministers, it bears witness with our spirits. We can know if something is not of the Father because it will not bear witness with our spirits.

I have a very precious Iranian friend who became a Christian, and at one time in his life, he used to be a shepherd. He told me that he could have a field full of sheep eating altogether, and as soon as he would yell to them, they would all immediately hear his voice and come to him. Why? Because the sheep know the voice of their master.

Manifesting God's Power on Earth

In the Bible, we see so many examples of how God worked through various people as they heard and were led by His Spirit. I have encountered many people who have amazing testimonies of what God has accomplished through them. I have a friend who died in a car crash after a drunk driver hit him. His wife and little girl were also killed. As his body laid on the highway, he looked down and saw himself along with the body of his wife and daughter. He then saw his wife and daughter begin to spin around, dancing with an angel on the highway. At that moment, he realized he was dead too. The next thing he saw was a beautiful ladder that looked like an escalator. His wife and daughter then began to ascend upward as the angel was guiding them. This man began to follow behind his wife and daughter, and the angel turned around, drew his sword, and said, "No, not you."

He said to the angel, "That's my wife and daughter, and I'm going with them."

The angel said to him, "You're going back because you are going to prevent World War III, and also, if you don't go back, the drunk driver who caused the accident will get away with it."

During his encounter with the angel, the angel took him over Russia, where he heard the people of Russia crying out to God. Then, the angel showed him the Magog invasion and things to come in our government along with a future strategy he would need to implement. After the angel finished showing him the things to come, he said to the angel, "Every bone in my body is broken. How can I go back?"

The angel said, "No problem." He pulled out his sword, touched the man's body, and instantly, he was made completely whole. Since he had already been pronounced dead at the scene, you can just imagine how freaked out the paramedics were when he came back to life, especially when he got up and began walking around as if nothing had happened.

"Each of us can change things here on earth when we hear and see things in the spirit."

At the time, this man was an attorney for the Navy, and he also taught at the war college. Later in his life, he actually did prevent World War III, and in fact, he's prevented many dangerous events. During his time at the Pentagon, he approached key generals, laying out a strategic plan telling them, "If you execute this action plan with the grid in Europe, it will stop or at least curtail a potential unwanted event," which very well could have been categorized as World War III. The generals and the people in this meeting thought, *Who is this guy?* But God had an appointed time and season for Bob to be instrumental in fulfilling His plan.

Later on, he went to the Pentagon. He foreknew this would happen as the angel showed him it would. While he was there, he had a significant influence on stopping more than two thousand attacks like 9/11 before they happened. Now, as we know, unfortunately, one got through. This is just some of this man's story. When I met him, he and I became friends. He is such a humble man. Initially, he didn't want to tell me his story. I am telling you his story because I want you to realize that each of us can change events here on earth when we hear and see in the spirit.

Once, I had seen two cities on fire in the spirit, and then I saw a third one on fire. The third one was not as bad as the other two. I had also seen a police car on fire in Atlanta, Georgia, during the riots that would happen. When I saw these things, I said to someone I knew, "When I come into your city to do a future show with Sid Roth, I will need to do these specific things so that I will be able to go through Atlanta without any issues."

Sure enough, when that visit happened, we saw that a police car was on fire in Atlanta, and he and others said, "Is this what you saw?"

I said "yes," and because I yielded to the Spirit, I could go through Atlanta without any issues.

This same thing happened with King Hezekiah and Isaiah, the prophet of the Lord. Isaiah spoke the prophecy of the Lord to King Hezekiah, and then he turned around to start leaving, and the Lord said, "Not so fast." Do you know why? Because Hezekiah had turned on his side, and he repented before Isaiah had even left. Isaiah hadn't even left the outer court of the king when God spoke to him. So what happened here? Did the prophet miss it, or was he a false prophet? No, he had heard correctly from God. See, this is where prophets make mistakes. We all have a will, and the outcome of events is conditional, according to the decisions we make.

God Is Looking for Those He Can Trust

When I was with Jesus for five hours in May 2020, I could see darkness coming that was to begin in September, lasting through the end of the year. Jesus said to me, "You have three months to implement all these different ministries." During this encounter, he also showed me that if we did not repent, turning to God, asking Him for help, and demanding righteousness and justice in this nation and on the earth, that this darkness He showed me would be allowed to come about. I even saw soldiers at the polls, and I saw the military going into cities, all before it happened. I saw troops being dispatched into downtown cities where they had cordoned off the whole area, and people weren't allowed to go into these locations unless they wanted to get shot. I was even shown a new disease and was given the name of it. It was an old disease that was revived.

The very next day, after I was shown these things, I read an article about how this particular disease was under investigation as possibly being discovered in a squirrel in Colorado; it was confirmed later it had appeared in another location in the US. Now, this particular disease was supposed to have been completely gone, but it resurfaced just as Jesus had shown me. When I read the article, I shared it with my wife and my staff. It is not a coincidence that I had been given the name of a disease that John G. Lake had entirely eradicated, and then it resurfaced again. I am serious. I know I'm not a professional at this; however, I am shown these kinds of things because Jesus knows He can trust me to change situations. He knows that I will pray and encourage the warriors to pray. When Jesus shows me something, He knows I won't just sit back and do nothing.

We must understand that when God knows He can trust you to pray and that you are determined in your heart to see His will come to pass, then He will show you things to come so that the outcome will be changed.

I believe one of the most profound things that Jesus said is found in Luke 11:1–2. Here, Jesus responds to a request made by one of His disciples who says, "Lord, teach us to pray."

Jesus answers, "When you pray, say: Our Father in heaven, hallowed be your name. Your kingdom come. Your will be done on earth as it is in Heaven." My memory of these verses growing up in a Presbyterian church was more of a religious experience because we prayed this prayer all the time, and for me, it really had no effect. These Scriptures have become words spoken in a religious setting, and because they are spoken all the time, they can become a kind of routine with no effect on people. This was my experience growing up. Jesus never went to any of the services there, and the Holy Spirit didn't either.

This reminds me of a story the president of one of the colleges I attended used to tell. He told me that when he was a little boy and had gotten baptized in the Holy Spirit, the church he attended kicked him out because of it. He then went outside the church, standing on the steps, crying about it, and this man walked up and asked, "What's wrong?"

And he said, "They just kicked me out of the church, and they won't let me back in." He then looked up to see the man talking to him, and it was Jesus.

Jesus replied, "I understand. They won't let me in either."

> *"We can pray to our heavenly Father, asking Him to reveal to us what is in heaven, the place where He lives and abides, which is His normal."*

Jesus hears and speaks words directly from the Father, and He tells these profound things to us. Selah. Pause and think about that. It is so amazing that we can pray to our heavenly Father, asking Him to reveal to us what is in heaven, where He lives and abides, which is His normal. In this revelation, we can partner with Him, bringing what is in heaven here into this realm. Isn't this precisely what Jesus taught His disciples? He taught them to bring God's will to the earth.

Now I'm not a Greek scholar, but I had professors who taught me that it is all about the verb tense. They explained that it is already in heaven and that through our prayers and declarations, we bring it to earth. When you bring heaven to earth, it changes you, but it should not stop there. It should then start to change your environment, your family, your work, and your church. When I was in heaven, I saw that one thing stopping us from bringing heaven to earth is that we are staring at a clock and a calendar as if we were waiting for something to happen. The truth is that it has already been done! It sounds too simple, right? But the gospel is simple, and it's good news.

It Is God's Will to Redeem Your Bloodline

Becoming mature in Christ is understanding that when you are manifesting heaven here on earth, some people will begin acting up around you, but that is because of the demons that have become part of them. The demons are manifesting, and you cannot take it personally. Once people are saved and the invisible beings are cast out, transformation will happen in their lives.

Some demons are not part of a person's soul; they are merely around the person. This type of demon is called a familiar spirit. Familiar spirits hang around people because they want to enforce the curse in their bloodline. These spirits do not want to leave their territory because that's their gig. They've been working a long time and are assigned to the bloodline. These same spirits made your grandpa act up. They are assigned to each generation, even your kids. So when you see your kids doing the same things that Grandpa did, you know these familiar spirits are enforcing these bad habits or addictions. You are the one who is supposed to break off the generational curse because it's not supposed to be transferred to any future generations. Whenever I tell people this truth, I can hear devils screaming. They don't want me to tell you these things, but I will tell you this because these devils are worthless and have no power.

> *"God believes in generations and genealogies, and He wants your offspring to be mighty on the earth."*

You absolutely must know how important your bloodline is to God. He believes in generations and genealogies, and He loves people, and He wants your offspring to be mighty on the earth. (See Psalm 112:1–2.) God intends for your offspring to prosper and to leave an amazing legacy for Jesus. He never intended for your offspring to be in jail or suffer from addictions. These addictions are real and these demon spirits are mean; they don't care, they're mad, and you need to break free from them and break the related curses. "I am the vine, you are the branches. He who abides in Me, and I in him, bears much fruit; for without Me, you can do nothing. If anyone does not abide in Me, he is cast out as a branch and is withered; and they gather them and throw them into the fire, and they are burned" (John 15:5–6).

Connected through the Vine

Jesus not only instructed us *how* to advance God's Kingdom here on the earth but He also went to a whole other level by explaining that you are connected to the Vine, which is connecting you directly to the life source—Jesus Himself. You receive your life flow through Jesus. In John 15:5, Jesus says that apart from Him, you can do nothing. What does *nothing* mean? Exactly that—it means nothing. The amazing truth is that when you are grafted into Him, you can do the opposite of nothing, which is everything.

In verses 7 and 8, Jesus goes onto say, "If you abide in Me, and My words abide in you, you will ask whatever you desire, and it shall be done for you. By this My Father is glorified, that bear much fruit; so you will be my disciples." Please pay careful attention to what I'm about to share with you as this is very important. The topic of these verses in chapter 15 of John is about fruit, but more than that, Jesus is revealing what the fruit represents. It is "prayer fruit," which means it's our answered prayers.

Do you get that? Answered prayer is the result, or the *fruit*, of you remaining in the Vine. And because you are the branch connected to the Vine, the branch bears much fruit, the kind of fruit that lasts. Beyond this, Jesus explained that as you abide in Him and His words abide in you, you can ask whatever you desire, and it will be yours. Now I want you to notice it doesn't say "whatever you need." It says, "whatever you desire." Need and desire are two different words in the original language. (See G2309 and H4270 in *The Blue Letter Bible*.)[2] As they say, one of these is not like the other. It shall

---

[2] "Lexicon :: Strong's G2309 – thelō," *Blue Letter Bible*, accessed on September 17, 2021, https://www.blueletterbible.org/lexicon/g2309/kjv/tr/0-1/. "Lexicon :: Strong's H4270 - maḥsôr," *Blue Letter Bible*, accessed on September 17, 2021, https://www.blueletterbible.org/lexicon/h4270/kjv/wlc/0-1/.

be done, period. When Jesus said, "whatever you desire," he was referring to something entirely different from what you need.

The devil will try and get in and tell you that you're not supposed to have all your wants and desires answered, and he will try and convince you to only be satisfied with what you need. Well, the thing is, you need to pay your bills every month, but that won't get you out of debt. Just meeting your bills each month is not out of debt; not having any bills would be out of debt.

"Delight yourself also in the Lord, and He shall give you the desires of your heart" (Psalm 37:4). So when looking at this verse in Psalms, does it say, "He will give you your needs"? No, it says He will give you your desires. "The Lord is my Shepherd; I shall not need"? No, "I shall not want." (See Psalm 23.) And why is this? It's because God does exceedingly above what you can ask or think. So whatever you ask or think, He will do even more than that. This is good news, which is the gospel, so let's agree to always preach that message!

I am really emphasizing this; however, I don't care if you stop being my friend over this because, you see, I'm not afraid to lose friends. Don't be afraid of losing friends just because you choose to live your life full of joy and because you are genuinely taking God at His Word. God wants His people full of joy, but you can't be full of joy if the devil has you bound in the financial world. The devil has completely taken over the financial system down here so that you have to deal with a go-between person in everything. Even with religion, you have to go through a middleman, such as a priest.

At one time, God had to lean on my wife and me to change in this area because He wanted us to know His normal, and now He wants me to lean on you and introduce you to His normal, too, which is to be debt-free. You are not supposed to be bound by anything. We are to owe no man anything except to love them. (See Romans 13:8.) This is also how we operate Warrior Notes; we won't do anything until the money comes in, but God always makes sure it comes.

Pruning Produces More Fruit

In John 15:2, Jesus explains that He prunes every branch that does not bear fruit so that it will bear fruit. We will go through some painful experiences during our Christian walk because God is getting rid of some things. Let me tell you a story about a friend of mine named Nick. Nick appeared on *It's Supernatural* with Sid Roth and told his story. He was diagnosed with incurable schizophrenia at the age of twenty, with the expectation from the doctor that he would be catatonic within the next few years. A schizophrenia diagnosis alone is more than enough. To add to that, he was deemed incurable, which meant that the medical community would never rescind this diagnosis because, as far as they were concerned, there was no reversing it.

Now, as Nick has explained it, one day, he found a flyer with a phone number on it for a Christian ministry. He called and spoke to a woman over the phone, who led him to receive Jesus. Shortly after that, through a series of events, Nick thought he found a place where he could serve the Lord, but it ended up being a cult. Once he escaped the cult, he started hearing voices telling him what to do. The voices constantly tormented him, even telling him to yell blasphemous things against God. The Lord then led him to a church where they prayed for him, and he experienced his first encounter of deliverance against these tormenting demons.

As Nick began learning about his authority in Christ, he listened to worship music, prayed, and told the demons they had to leave. Finally, over a period of three years, Nick was delivered from over a thousand demons. He tells the story of how he repeatedly walked around his mom's swimming pool playing Christian music, commanding the demons to leave until he finally became free.

As Nick continued believing God and walking through deliverance, his personality slowly began to change, and the real him started to emerge. When those devils left, parts of himself that weren't really him left too. But the story doesn't end there. After Nick went through learning his identity and authority in Christ, he went back and worked as an administrator at the same behavioral healthcare provider where he used to receive mental health services. He now testifies of what God has done in his life, bringing glory to Him. What a testimony he has! Yes, Nick went through a lot in his journey, but God completely restored his life.

As part of Nick's testimony, he also shares that before he was set free, he met a few people that told him Christians couldn't have a demon. But he told them, "Well, I know I do, and come on, you know I do too." Interestingly, many people still believe this.

What You Believe Will Become Evident

God desires that you bear much fruit, so some things will be pruned out of your life, and along the way, you may discover that some personality traits really aren't yours. You may find that you inherited some things or they were passed down to you through familiar spirits. I know that this is a very unpopular subject, and when I speak about this topic, I look for the Pharisees to show up and say, "Who do you think you are?"

You see, demon spirits can gain access to your soul realm, which will cause you to think differently. If you accept these ugly thoughts about yourself, you will begin to manifest them. Quite simply put, *what you believe is what you will manifest*. As soon as you realize this is happening, you need to acknowledge it and cast those demons out. I don't mean you cast them aside as some churches present it; I mean to follow Jesus's instructions, which is to drive them out, push them away, and be violent with them. Now, you can either listen to me or think I'm crazy. If you don't follow the instructions of Jesus, you will come back in a year, saying that you still have a problem.

See, you need to get rid of these invisible friends because they are not your friends. You do not have to be thrown down and spit up green soup to know you have a demon. The truth is that the demon will have you. You may have heard the same thing that Nick did: Christians can't have a demon. But a demon *can* have a Christian because, although your spirit is saved, you can still experience demonic manifestation. I am tired of ministries not addressing this.

Come on, now. We need to grow up and be accountable. We need to admit that something is wrong. Certain things that are being taught are just not working. I am saying these things because I want you to walk in total freedom, and I want you to live out exactly what God pronounced over you even before you were born. I want you to fulfill your destiny—all of it. However, if you can't resolve some of the discrepancies in your life, it's time to get violent with the devil because these evil spirits have to break off you. You must take the authority to remove their influence or involvement in your life.

You Are Not a Victim

One way you will know that evil spirits influence your life is that they will affect your emotions and the way you think. Due to their influence, you will react a certain way when specific actions or events happen to you or when certain things are said. They want to push your buttons. They can even program you in rejection cycles. They will work on other people that have allowed them access to their lives to repeatedly reject you. They know exactly what to do to get a person to speak hurtful, untrue things to you and keep them doing this in cycles or even on a schedule.

I'm not kidding you. You can chart it; it's like clockwork. I could not believe it when I saw this. Once I realized this, I put an end to it. I started laughing every time that demon would come, and I guess I hurt it because he has not come back anymore. After all, I'm not a victim, and neither are you. Trust me when I say, some demons hope you don't believe what I'm telling you here. Just know, once you realize and enforce the truth and you stand believing that you are not a victim anymore, they have to go.

All of Heaven Believes That You Cannot Fail

As a child of God, your spirit does not have any failure in it. When you were born again, you became a new creation, and the Spirit of the living God came to live inside you. Furthermore, Jesus is continually interceding on your behalf (Romans 8:34). Even the angels that have read your books in heaven and that have been assigned to you never think you will fail. They are just looking for cooperation from you. Listen, Jesus told the disciples that when He returned to His Father, He would send the Holy Spirit, who would guide them into all truth as John 16 says, so what are you concerned about?

You must realize the truth: angels around you are enforcing the blessing. The Holy Spirit inside you is enforcing the blessing, bringing you into victory. God always sees you as an overcomer, and the Holy Spirit has never doubted you. Jesus has never had a wrong thought about you. He has never thought that you wouldn't win, ever. The Holy Spirit has never thought you would fail, ever. Your angel has never thought you would have a mission failure. Your Father, who wrote your book in heaven, never, ever thought you would fail. The Trinity doesn't think that way, and neither do the angels or anyone else in heaven.

All of heaven is cheering for you, saying, "Don't slow down, keep going!" So together with them, we will have reached the fulfillment of God's heart in the coming age. One day, we will all be together in heaven, and each one of us will be able to tell our story of what we did for Jesus and how He saw His desire released on His enemy. This is the absolute truth and not a bedtime story.

Friends of God

A friend of God is when God likes you so much that He lets you in on what He's doing, just like He did with Abraham. (See Genesis 18:16–33.) God decided to consult with Abraham about His plans regarding what was going on in Sodom and Gomorrah. But see, it was all a setup because God was in a pickle. He was in trouble. God would not destroy Sodom and Gomorrah because Lot was there, and he wasn't supposed to be. Lot was also included in the covenant, and God will not break His covenant. (See Psalm 89:34.)

God let Abraham know about the situation in Sodom and Gomorrah, and Abraham brought his concern before the Lord regarding the righteous in the city. God would not destroy the city without first revealing His plan to Abraham and inviting him to converse with Him. Many cannot accept this, but didn't God also do the same thing with Moses? You see, this is how you know you are a friend of God. He will tell you something that He will do and you say, "No, Lord, this would be against you. This would not be right." It's a setup because He wants to develop dialogue. Why? Because we have authority. Stay with me here. When Abraham found out what the situation was from God, he immediately started thinking, *Oh my gosh, Lot is there.* He began negotiating with God. In the end, the angels went to get Lot and his wife and bring them safely out of the city before God destroyed it.

"So that we may no longer be children, tossed to and fro by the waves and carried about by every wind of doctrine, by human cunning, by craftiness in deceitful schemes" (Ephesians 4:14). This passage describes some of the ministries we see in operation today. Paul explained here that we are no longer children; we are adults, and since we are adults, we will pursue and adhere to sound doctrine. As adults, we can be a friend of God, relying on Him as our Father. As for me, I want to be a part of what God is doing on the earth, and I know you do too. For that to happen, we must be walking as mature sons and daughters so that God will come and pull back veils to reveal to us what He is doing. However, He needs our permission to do so. Now some religious leaders would say, "God doesn't need to communicate or receive our input regarding anything that He is planning to do." But if that were true, why did He go to Moses or Abraham? Or why did He try talking Cain out of what he was about to do ? God tried to reason with and coach Cain, showing him what he needed to do so that he would be accepted (Genesis 4) I think that we can conclude that a friend of God is someone who God can trust, and He will go to them and show them things. He wants to communicate with you as a friend would, pulling back the veil, revealing His plans.

"Then the Lord said to Moses, 'Leave this place, you and the people you brought up out of Egypt, and go up to the land I promised on oath to Abraham, Isaac and Jacob, saying, "I will give it to your descendants"" (Exodus 33:1 NIV). Here we see that God wasn't calling the children of Israel *His* people because He said to Moses, "the people you brought up out of Egypt." God said this because they had rebelled against Him, and their hearts were set on evil (Exodus 32:22).

God told Moses, "Now, therefore, let Me alone, that My wrath may burn hot against them and I may consume them" (Exodus 31:10). At that point, Moses reminded God that they were His people and that He had made a covenant with them and had promised to bring them out into the land of promise (Exodus 21:11–14). So, we can see that Moses was speaking to God as a friend and God was listening and talking to him as a friend. God was saying, "Look, these people give me a rash, so leave me be so I can just destroy them." But after Moses spoke with God, He then revealed to Moses that He could not be with them because they were stiff-necked, unthankful, unbelieving, and rebellious people. But God heard what Moses said and sent an angel with them into the land of promise (Exodus 32:34). Here, we see what it looked like when Moses and God talked as friends. God listened to what Moses had to say, and God then changed His mind.

A Foundation Built on God's Character

In Hebrews 3:18–19; 4:1, Paul writes to the body, reminding them that their forefathers did not enter into the rest of God or inherit the promise because of their unbelief. He then says not to be like them. Friends of God have learned how to enter into His rest, and from there, He communes with them.

"Your faith must rest in God's character
and not in your ability to believe."

You need to understand that your faith must rest in God's character and not in your ability to believe. Let's pause here for a moment and think about this. I trust in God's character, and I believe that what He says is the truth as He cannot lie. I also believe that He is able and willing to perform anything that He has said or anything that is written in His Word. If He says I am healed, I don't care if I am limping; I am healed. This is how I've systematically seen different parts of my body miraculously healed, one by one. It's too late for anyone to tell me that it won't happen because, as far as I'm concerned, it's already done, and it will manifest in the natural. If the devil says anything, you can know that the opposite of what he says will always be the truth. This is because he is the father of lies, and there is no truth in him (John 8:44).

Part of becoming a mature Christian is renewing your mind in the Word of God and allowing Him to reveal any false teachings that you have embraced. One of the reasons the body of Christ has not walked in the revelation that we are children of God, let alone the truth that you can be a friend of God, is because of these wrong belief systems. God wants to reveal to you any false teachings you have believed so that you can walk in the truth.

"I said, 'You are gods, And all of you are children of the Most High'" (Psalm 82:6). This is another example of a truth that is not talked about in ministries. In John 10, Jesus quoted this Scripture in response to the Pharisees and said, "Is it not written in your law, 'I said, you are gods?' If He called them gods, to whom the word of God came, (and the scripture cannot be broken)" (John 10:34–35). When God said, "you are gods" (with a little g), the word god also means "judges." When I quote this verse, some people are afraid. But listen, that's only a problem when you don't rightly divide the truth. Part of what was said here is that we are judges. A spiritual man can make judgments about all things, but he is not subject to anyone's judgment (1 Corinthians 2:15). That's in the Bible, too, right?

Commentaries, such as Matthew Henry's, don't usually touch on most of these verses about the divine nature because of their religious thinking. What I am telling you here is so important. Think about it. With religious thinking, could you ever be a friend of God, or could you ever inherit what Jesus inherited? With everything that Jesus obtained for His children, I want the body to realize that we have been left out. Not everything that He paid for on our behalf is being taught. I don't want to tiptoe around these matters. I want you to know everything that Jesus has for you.

Religion Will Keep You from the Truth

"I will no longer talk much with you, for the ruler of this world is coming, and he has nothing in Me" (John 14:30). Religion makes you afraid to take a step into the truth so that devils don't leave. When you don't know the truth, the devil will have something in you. When Jesus said, "The ruler of the world is coming, and he has nothing in me," He meant that the devil has no fleshhook or a place to hook Him. As you learn the truth and walk in it, the Holy Spirit will begin to modify your personality by pruning it, and then you will become a mature child, able to receive from God.

Now what about the area of giving? It seems you hear a lot about giving, but see, that's religion. The message of giving ought to be built on a foundation that you give because you love God and honor Him. You also give because He has given to you, but you must also have an understanding of how to receive from God

I recently came out with two books simultaneously, *You Can Hear God's Voice* and *Supernatural Finances*, which address receiving from God. The truth is that you do not give to God so that he will give to you because he has already given to you; you only need to receive and then honor Him back. I pray that you are getting a revelation of this truth and that it genuinely unravels any religious thinking you may have been believing. The tithe was never yours; the Lord said, "The tithe is mine." (See Leviticus 27:30.) It's a test. The real question is, will you honor God with your tithe?

It's kind of like the movie *Willy Wonka and the Chocolate Factory*. Remember when Charlie was being tested at the end to see if he would take the chocolate out of the factory after they told him he couldn't? The chocolate belonged to Mr. Wonka; it wasn't Charlie's to take. Because he passed the test, he inherited the whole factory. He became an heir. Here we are, arguing about whether tithing is Old Testament or New Testament, which has nothing to do with it. It is a test. As I'm writing this, I feel the power of God so strongly. God wants you to get this; He wants you to receive everything He has for you.

Power to Become Sons of God

"But those who embraced him and took hold of his name, he gave authority to become the children of God!" (John 1:12 TPT) This passage says one of the most profound things written in the Bible. The Greek word for "power" in this Scripture is *exousia* which means "authority."[3] It is not referencing the other translation and meaning of the word power, *dynamis*, meaning "dynamite."[4] I have Greek friends that keep me straight if I say it wrong. It becomes life-

---

[3] "Lexicon :: Strong's G1849 – exousia," *Blue Letter Bible*, accessed September 17, 2021, https://www.blueletterbible.org/lexicon/g1849/kjv/tr/0-1/.

[4] "Lexicon :: Strong's G1411 – dynamis," *Blue Letter Bible*, accessed September 17, 2021, https://www.blueletterbible.org/lexicon/g1411/kjv/tr/0-1/.

changing when we grasp the revelation that God has given us the power to become sons of God. An example would be a person that weighs a hundred pounds with the authority to stop a truck. It's not about your size; it's about the power or the authority you have been given when you believed in the name of Jesus and were born of the Spirit of God.

> *"Since the world will not comprehend the light of God in you, you will meet resistance."*

John 1:1 says, "In the beginning was the Word, and the Word was with God, and the Word was God." We understand that there is no difference between the Word (Jesus) and God. "He was in the beginning with God. All things were made through Him, and without Him nothing was made that was made. In Him was life, and that life was the light of men, and the light shines in the darkness, and the darkness did not comprehend it" (John 1:2–5).

Since you are light in this world, you need to expect that darkness will not comprehend you. Since the world will not comprehend the light of God in you, you will meet resistance. The benefit is that you become God's friend when you are persecuted. In Matthew 5:10–12, Jesus told us to be full of joy and jump up and down when we are persecuted. Why did He say this? It's because you are counted. So when you are persecuted, do what I do—become excited!

Don't you find it interesting that the religious system persecuted Jesus? Those people gave Him trouble. Well, when you preach the pure gospel, all of a sudden, lines are drawn, and your people turn on you. In 1 John 2:19, Paul explained that those who left us were never with us.

Love Equals Obedience

In John 14:15, Jesus says, "If you love me, keep my commandments." Don't miss this—Jesus is saying, love is the *same as* obedience. Now I ask you, how does love equate to being the same as obedience? We don't just tell Jesus we love Him; we show Him that we love Him. As I am writing this, I just had a thought. If more people had a revelation of this truth, then maybe we would have an increase of Jesus appearing to people. Words are cheap. In heaven, no one disobeys God. No one in heaven takes what God says for granted. Even when an angel is speaking, they are speaking from the very heart of God because everything has an order in heaven.

The Ending of the Healing Revivals

When I was at Rhema Bible College, Kenneth Hagin used to say that the reason the healing revivals stopped was that people were trying to make it work on their own. At one time, the Spirit of God was not moving in those healing gifts anymore. When the Spirit of God stopped, those men got into error, and they died early. I mean, some of them were only in their thirties. Part of obeying the Spirit is discerning if the cloud stops moving, then you don't move either.

Once, Kenneth Hagan told me that he and Oral Roberts had a conversation when all that was happening, and they said to each other, "All these guys will be gone, and we'll make it through." That was when God told them to go to Tulsa and start a school. Unfortunately, when you look at those who were at the forefront of the healing revivals, all of them died early, even William Branham. That was not God's doing. I read Branham's journal, who wrote that his angel showed up after a revival meeting, and Branham stood there with his arms crossed because he was mad at the angel. That went on for six months.

But see, in these instances, God becomes slandered. Everyone at those meetings thought that the angel would come and take him to the person's past, showing him everything. For instance, he might say, "I saw you in your yellow dress at age fourteen on a swing." After saying this, people thought, *Okay, God will heal them right now*. But instead, the people began to believe that God didn't want the person healed. Branham paced in the meetings, waiting on the angel to show up. But he didn't because God wouldn't send him because the men were not doing what God was telling them to do.

Another time, a newspaper reporter infiltrated one of the meetings to try and trick Branham. He wrote a fake disease on his card. When it was handed to Branham, he read it and said, "I don't see anything wrong with you." He then said, "Give me that card. Thus says the Lord, 'You shall have this disease.'" The reporter later died of that illness. This is an example of how someone gets off course from God, and he even died early when a drunk driver hit him. Branham laid his hands on his wife, who was next to him when the accident occurred, and she was healed, but he died. This scenario can create a discrepancy in your mind. You may think, *Why didn't that angel show up for him at the accident? Was he on a lunch break*? This can happen when you don't know the whole story. See, the angel knew that Branham was not doing what he was told.

Brother Hagin and Oral Roberts lived out their entire lives because they made the switch. No one is perfect, and I'm not here to judge anyone. But I'm telling you, those two survived the healing revival and stayed alive, which was great because none of the others did. We all needed those men to teach us, right? Since you love God, obey His Word, and He promises his angels will come and move in with you, bringing their furniture.

CHAPTER 5

A Love for God's Word

My soul keeps your testimonies,
and I love them exceedingly.
—Psalms 119:167

One of David's strongest traits was that he was a worshipper, but he also loved God's Word. Even though he made mistakes, he loved his heavenly Father, and God knew him as his friend. Psalm 119 is so unique and beautiful. I go through this chapter a lot because it gets me flowing in the love of God and honoring His word. I ask the students of Warrior Notes to read Psalms 119 and then write out what the Lord speaks to them because it will bring correction. And we all certainly need correction.

We need a course correction so that we end up at our destination. God's Word is not the word of faith movement. This particular chapter in Psalms reveals that when God says something, He means it. There is no difference between Him and what He says. If you know His Word, then you know His personality, which I found to be true in heaven. Jesus is exactly like the red letters we read in the Bible. This should not have been a surprise to me, but it was. Jesus was quoting Himself for forty-five minutes, and I didn't even know some of the verses Jesus was saying to me. I thought I was a scholar, but when He talked, He spoke with true authority, and every word Jesus said, He meant.

Here in this realm, it's rare to find someone who will keep their word. As a result, we're conditioned not to take it seriously when someone says, "I love you." Years ago, when I was eating at Denny's after work one evening, I met this guy and spoke to him about Lord. The power of God hit him, and he got saved. I led him in the baptism of the Holy Spirit, and he began praying in tongues. He then asked me if he could stay overnight at my place for one night. So I told him that I needed to get up early and go to school in the morning and that he would have to be out before I left. He agreed; however, before he left, he unlocked one of the windows at my place, and then he came back later and stole all my money, which I had held aside for my tuition. If I didn't have the money for tuition, they would not allow me to go back to school because they were so strict. You had to pay your money ahead of time.

I called the police, and of course, I could identify him, so they got his prints and his sneaker imprint outside of my window. The police told me they would go and pick him up if I would press charges, but I said no. At that time, the police officers in Tulsa were mainly Christians, so they understood me when I explained that the guy had gotten saved the night before. I just didn't feel right about pressing charges, but I was upset. I ended up working extra hours because I had three jobs. My finances increased, so I was able to make up all the financial loss somehow. A couple of weeks later, I was at a traffic light, and the same guy pulled up next to me on his brand-new motorcycle. Well, it was really my motorcycle, but I will see him in heaven.

Do people really love and appreciate you? See, the guy isn't going to hell, but he will work on going to hell if he doesn't become transformed in his mind through the Word of God. His spirit is saved, but his words are cheap. When those kinds of things happen to you, you can get to the point where you don't trust anyone. The problem is that it will bleed over into your relationship with your heavenly Father. How do we relate to someone we have never met? He's invisible, but He's the only true God, and He does exist, and we get to know Him through His Word. I also know that the majority of people are not like the man I mentioned. I have met some people that I know in my spirit are humble and good and will keep their word, and when I meet someone like that, I sometimes cry because I know they are a rare treasure.

I noticed when I was with Jesus that every Word He said, He meant and that's who He is as a person; it's not just a trait of His. He's not just faithful as an adjective. He *is* faithful. He's the noun. He's Faithful and True. That's His name, and it's written on his leg. (See Revelation 19:11.) You'll see it when He comes back on His horse. That's why it's so important to love His Word because by doing so, you are loving God.

You Don't Need to Storm the Gates of Heaven

Jesus said, "And when you pray, do not use vain repetitions as the heathen do. For they think that they will be heard for their many words" (Matthew 6:7). Instead, He says, "Ask, and it will be given to you; seek, and you will find; knock, and it will be opened to you" (Matthew 7:7). Some people quote the parable of the man who kept bothering his friend to get some bread because if you just keep asking, you will get what you need. However, I want you to understand that the man asking for bread was an unjust person (Luke 11:5–8). Jesus told me that if I would learn and know the Word of God, getting it down into my heart, I would be able to cut my prayer time down by 85 percent. Yeah, He explained that busting down the gates of heaven is not needed. You don't have to storm the gates of heaven; you can storm the gates of hell. Everyone is afraid of the devil and hell, but you don't have to break down the gates of heaven.

I have fasted and prayed in tongues for hours and hours, including fasting twenty-one days several different times. I have prayed in tongues all the time, and when I say all the time, I mean all the time. Just two years ago, I prayed in tongues for three days, twenty-four hours a day without eating, and my wife was there with me. On the third day, an angel came, and it changed my life forever. The same anointing and power of that twenty-one-day fast is on me. Can you believe that? What happened? I matured. How did I mature? I learned God's character by His Word. Jesus told me that my prayers went directly to the Father. I don't have to pray in tongues for twelve hours to reach my Father, and neither do you. We don't need to go through any saints or any of Jesus's relatives. We can go directly to Jesus.

"At that time, you won't need to ask me for anything. I tell you the truth, you will ask the Father directly, and he will grant your request because you use my name" (John 16:23 NLT). When I was in the throne room, I didn't get to see our Father's face, but what was there was so amazing. Even the beams around the throne and above the throne were so wonderful. Many amazing things were going on there with so much authority that you do not even want to talk. When God does speak, everyone knows it, and He gets what He says and what He wants, and so does Jesus.

Jesus also gets what He wants down here through His body. He is waiting for His enemies to become His footstool. (See Hebrews 10:13.) That happens through the church, right? So if we permit things down here, they will be permitted; if we forbid them, they will be forbidden (See Matthew 18:18 NLT). When I encounter God's normal, I am encountering His Word, and it is absolute.

I have asked people what challenges they are dealing with, and I am up to around fifty-four titles for books that I still have to write. I want to write books based on struggles people have, so I have about fifty more books yet to begin because I'm filling in the ditches of people's lives so that there are no more ditches. This is what God does; He preemptively fixes things for you. God keeps the answers in His Word, so we just need to learn how to relate to God, knowing His intent and personality, understanding what He means by what He says in His Word.

Jesus' Personality

"So shall My word be that goes forth from My mouth; it shall not return to Me void, but it shall accomplish what I please, and it shall prosper in the thing for which I sent it" (Isaiah 55:11). God speaks, sending out His Word, and His intentions are fulfilled. It doesn't come back void; whatever its intent was to accomplish, it does just that. That is the way He is. You may think you will like certain people until you meet them, but then you realize that they might not fit your personality. Jesus could be that way to you because you think He will have tea with you and watch HBO. I can tell you that the wise thing to do if Jesus shows up is to let Him do all the talking. Turn everything off and cancel your schedule. Because we are so busy, it's tough if that show you want to watch comes on at seven o'clock and Jesus shows up at a quarter to seven.

I remember the night when I woke up to an invisible entity kicking me and calling my name. I rolled over and then fell back asleep. I couldn't believe I did that. Well, I didn't have another visitation for years. Why would I have done that? It's because I was becoming lukewarm; I was allowing my troubles to consume me. I wasn't sober-minded, knowing that at any moment, Jesus or heaven could come and visit me, speak with me, and help me. See, I had been involved in a certain situation, and I didn't know until later that it was not a good idea. The angel that came that night was trying to wake me up and warn me, but I missed the visitation. Everything worked out, but it's still sobering to me today. I told the Lord, "If I had known, I would have never been involved in that situation," but Jesus told me that was why the angel had come that night—to warn me. I know that I never want to miss another visitation.

God Never Fails

After the fall of man, the world began to deteriorate. Many of the problems that we deal with now did not exist when God created the world. For instance, we now have microscopic germs in our bodies. Additionally, prior to the flood, everything lived longer. Things like germs and yeast could not exist because the atmosphere was so oxygen-rich that nothing unhealthy could live in pure oxygen.

Before God created the earth, He already knew that man would fall and interbreed. When He created the earth, He also created caverns under the earth's crust that contained water. He told me this was an extra move because He knew He would have to flood the earth. Prior to the fall, it never rained (Genesis 2:5–6). God planned and placed a water source underneath the earth's crust. For rain to occur, you need condensation nuclei in the air and dust particles to be charged; as this happens, water collects in the clouds, forming water drops. Since there was no pollution at that time, this would not have happened.

God, foreknowing what would happen, planned ahead because He never fails. Are you starting to understand that?

When it came time to flood the earth, He released the water from the underground caverns. When it burst forth, it was so strong, it shot up thousands of feet, taking dirt along with it, and then bingo, we had clouds. Then it rained for forty days.

When this happened, the magnetic field of the earth changed, and everything shifted. The fruit of the vine then had yeast on it because the fruit was fermented. Do you remember that the world was perfect before the fall, and nothing deteriorated? Well, fermentation is a form of deterioration. Alcohol is formed from the yeast. So alcohol has to do with the fall, just as sin has to do with the fall. That is why they had unleavened bread (bread without yeast) to represent bread without sin. This is why Jesus said to beware of the leaven of the Pharisees; He was talking about the yeast in their teaching (Matthew 16:6).

When Noah got drunk, it was not because he drank a large quantity of the fruit of the vine; it was because it had deteriorated. People today are fighting about whether they can drink. We have plants that people say must be all right to smoke because God gave them to us. Oh sure, why don't you pet an alligator and ride a lion too? I can tell you I wouldn't want a person that smoked that plant to be flying my jet. When I worked for Southwest Airlines, we had passengers get on board all the time and ask, "Hey, can I fly today?" I answered, "Sure, but I'm going home if you're flying."

Remember, Noah got drunk, and then some very bad things happened. This type of situation is why Ephesians 5:18 says, "And be not drunk with wine, wherein is excess; but be filled with the Spirit" (KJV). The spiritual representation of wine is that of the blood of Jesus and the Holy Spirit. See, the blood and the water agree in that both of them wash you. The representation of wine today isn't the same as it was then. Our world keeps getting to the place where everything is deteriorating as a result of the fall.

Eat God's Word One Slice at a Time

"Then Jesus said to them, 'Most assuredly, I say to you, Moses did not give you the bread from heaven, but My Father gives you the true bread from heaven'" (John 6:32). God's Word is the bread and Jesus's blood is the wine, but this has nothing to do with sin, which is the yeast. We focus on the fact that Jesus drank wine. First Timothy 5:23 tells us to drink a little wine for our stomachs. But we must know just how sacred communion is supposed to be. Paul explained that many are sick and even die early because they don't discern the Lord's body when they sit at the table and take communion (Corinthians 11:29–30). Communion is a representation. Jesus is the true bread from heaven, and He gives life to the world. This is why Jesus said that to be a part of Him, you must eat His flesh because bread represents His body (John 6:53).

Jesus told me to eat His Word like bread, and He told me not to eat the whole loaf at once but to eat one slice at a time. He explained to me that it was better to study one sentence at a time and eat it until I felt it go down and hit the bottom of my spirit. Now, it might take a couple of minutes to do that, or it might take an hour. I have had more visitations by myself in my room with no one there, and I've been healed. God healed my eyes, and all I was doing was meditating on one verse. The glory came in, and I was healed, and your eyes aren't just healed at sixty years old. It was God as I sat there and meditated on one verse.

I have certain books and chapters that I read all the time; I meditate in the book of John, one sentence at a time from John 14 to 17. Then I go to 1 Corinthians 2, all of Ephesians,

Genesis, and Hebrews. Perhaps someday I will get it, and I can go on; that's what Jesus told me. Just those verses alone have given me enough to run on for the rest of my life. Jesus is the Word; He's the bread that came down from heaven. Jesus said, "Man shall nor live by bread alone, but by every word that proceeds from the mouth of God" (Matthew 4:4). I wouldn't trade anything for the freedom that I feel right now with the Spirit of God being upon me.

> *"We eat and we drink of the Lord, and He becomes part of us, and then one day, He becomes all of us."*

The Word of God Is Active and Living

The Holy Spirit is the referee of peace; He commands peace, and He speaks peace. He also enforces the covenant and the blessing. He's more like Jesus than you think. He's not a bird that hovers over you; He's a person that's like Jesus, and He has the same authority, and He wants to speak and manifest through you. I have found that meditating on God's Word is where it's at. Meditating on God's Word is the cool thing that is coming back. One day, you'll realize what I'm saying is true because we've turned much of the Christian life into a carnival when it's actually very simple.

We eat and we drink of the Lord, and He becomes part of us, and then one day, He becomes all of us. We then start to change our environment around us and begin to change history. We make things right because of God's compassion in us and because it pours out through us. We reach out, and we heal the sick. We drive out devils, and we preach the good news. It all shifts because God has His home in you. We live from every word that comes from His mouth. We drink of the Spirit of God; we drink of Him. I drink of Him, and I can feel the River of Life. When I drink of the Spirit, I get drunk in the Spirit. He is reigning in my life, and He is reigning inside you.

Jesus Wants to Affect Your World

Jesus wants to come out through you and affect your world. I have been taken to the future many times and then brought back. Then I watch it play out, and I won't let you continue in the wrong direction when Jesus Christ has sent Himself and healed you. He sent Himself, and He is the Word.

"For the Word of God is living and powerful, and sharper than any two-edged sword, piercing even to the division of soul and spirit, and of joints and marrow, and is a discerner of the thoughts and intents of the heart" (Hebrews 4:12). The Word is the only thing that can separate the soul and the spirit and the marrow on the inside. Now, read that verse out loud. Can you sense the fire burning inside your spirit? What's happening is that the Word will show you the difference between your psyche or the psychological part of you, your soul, and your spirit.

Your spirit does not know any defeat and doesn't doubt or fear. It's the only part of you that knows everything will be just fine. When everything around us begins to tear apart, my wife and I start laughing because we have inside information that comes from our spirits. We have a witness of the Spirit, no matter what is going on around us. That's because the Word of God dwells richly in us, and it's a person and His name is Jesus.

The Lord's Supper Is a Spiritual Communion

"When you take communion,
something spiritual happens."

Your heavenly Father will not lie to you because He's not a man that He should lie (Numbers 23:19). This means when He says something, it's absolutely true, and you need to reinforce what He says. Even though the facts say that you are sick, the absolute truth is that you were healed, and it's already been done. It just needs to manifest.

You also need to drink and eat from the heavenly realm, for this is your life. Why would Jesus say, "Take, eat; this is my body which is broken for you; do this in remembrance of Me" (Matthew 26:26)? Paul wrote the same thing in 1 Corinthians and said, "Do this as often as you can until Jesus comes" (1 Corinthians 11:26). You honor that because it's a holy time; it's not make-believe or a children's program. This is very sacred. You remember the night when Jesus was betrayed, and you honor Him. You use physical elements to represent a spiritual communion, but when you take communion, something spiritual happens, something inside you. I'm more a part of Him than I ever have been, but I might only be halfway there.

When You Give Yourself Fully to God

We were previously in Dalton, Georgia, and I told the crowd of 750 people, "You'll know when I have fully given myself over because the whole place will be on the floor and will not be able to get back into their chairs." See, I was in the future, and I already know what will happen in meetings when I turn myself completely over to Him. People will be sitting, and they will just fall over without a word being said. He wants to do this to get the bride ready. I saw that as soon as people came inside the meetings, they would get saved and healed. I saw Christians coming to the meetings because the glory of the Father had come in, and it was drawing them.

When I yield fully to the Spirit, I can hear the Spirit saying things about me that you'd be jealous of, but see, He's doing the same thing with you. He's talking you up. He's telling you about who you really are. People are not aware of this, but He talks about where you're going. He's calling the things that are not as though they were. Right now, in your spirit, the Holy Spirit is calling you faithful, calling you transformed, calling you a prophetic voice for this nation and this generation. The Holy Spirit is talking about what will happen tomorrow and the next day, in the next year, and all the plans He has for you. I'm not kidding you.

I've had people translate my tongues that knew the language. They told me exactly what I was saying, and within twenty-four hours, the times, places, and the people that I spoke about all happened like clockwork even though in the natural it didn't look like it would happen. The Holy Spirit knows tomorrow before we do, and He's inside you; it's a local call. So when you feel the Holy Spirit burning inside you, you know that the Holy Spirit has enough fuel from the Word. When you're ignited and when you burn, you can do anything. You just have to learn to walk like this all the time from the moment you get up. Can you get up and walk out there all day, staying in step with the Holy Spirit?

The Supernatural Word of God

The key to encountering God's normal is framing your world by the Word of God and then eating it. Now is the time to advance into deeper spiritual truths, which means you must go to Hebrews and live there. I listened to Hebrews over and over again for years; in fact, all the years that you didn't know me and some of them that you have. Every time before I speak anywhere, I listened to the book of Hebrews with my earbuds in while I quoted it out loud. I do this because the Lord told me it's a supernatural book just like they all are. He also told me that Genesis is especially supernatural because it was given to Moses by angels. See, Moses wrote Genesis, but he didn't live in Genesis, so it was given to him on the mountain by angels. I have found that Genesis is also a profound book with many hidden truths in it that you might even see played out in the next year. Hebrews is like that too; it doesn't have a known author.

I want to take you into some advanced spiritual truths here and give you some secrets. If you read Hebrews and eat it as bread, you will go deeper in spiritual truths than you ever thought possible. Don't you want to know what I saw on the other side? I have given you hints already as to which other books and chapters of the Bible to begin with; however, when you continue eating the Word like bread and it becomes part of you, then you begin to know God and go onto maturity, which is where I want to be and where I want everyone else to be.

The Meat of The Word Is for Mature Believers

For though by this time you ought to be teachers, you need someone to teach you again the first principles of the oracles of God; and you have come to need milk and not solid food. For everyone who partakes only of milk is unskilled in the word of righteousness, for he is a babe. But solid food belongs to those who are [b]of full age, that is, those who by reason of use have their senses exercised to discern both good and evil. (Hebrews 5:12–14)

What Paul talked about in the previous passage is still happening today. You can see why people become deceived because he's telling you right here. When I was in heaven, I saw this; we, as Christians, are supposed to be the sharpest living people on earth. Look at the Scripture where Jesus said, "We are to be as wise as a serpent but as innocent as a dove" (Matthew 10:16). The whole idea is that a snake always rises to strike when you approach it, but he will first warn you. But you have to be as innocent as a dove. You must know that you need to be prepared to respond at any moment. Everywhere I go, I know my exits out of a building.

I know what I will do if I were to face an emergency because I was trained that way. I always have my car keys ready before I leave out the door. I check my tires, I check if anyone is underneath the car, and when I pull up to a gas station, I look around everywhere. When I go over to the pump, I pull on the credit card slot to make sure it's not a fake one where they are trying to steal your data. Everywhere I go, I look around to identify any possibly suspicious people. Why? Because I don't trust anyone.

I always know where my wallet and my passport are, and I know where my weapon is. I keep it in the same place every time so it never gets lost. Jesus taught me to be this way because He said that's what the parable of the snake and the dove was all about. You are as innocent as a dove, but you're as shrewd as a snake. In other words, a snake doesn't trust anyone because he's at a disadvantage. When you're constantly being stalked by a wild animal, like a mountain lion, they take the high ground because they are looking down at you. They're not at the same level as you are; they're high up, tracking you.

Your Promotion to the Next Level

David killed the giant after he had already killed the bear and the lion. You know the story. David went to bring food to his brothers, and when he got there, he couldn't believe his eyes. King Saul and all of the army were hiding as this giant was just railing at everyone. David said, "What will be done for the man who kills this Philistine and removes this disgrace from Israel? Who is this uncircumcised Philistine that he should defy the armies of the living God?" (1 Samuel 17:26 NIV). They were looking for any numbskull they could throw out there. You know, someone they could throw under the bus.

When they told Saul that someone was inquiring about killing Goliath, the king told them to bring this person to him. When King Saul saw that David was a boy, he told him that he couldn't go up against the giant. David responded to the king, "Your servant used to keep his father's sheep, and when a lion or a bear came and took a lamb out of the flock, I went out after it and struck it, and delivered the lamb from its mouth; and when it arose against me, I caught it by its beard, and struck and killed it" (1 Samuel 17:34–35). Did you catch that? David said he *used* to keep his Father's sheep. He saw his day of promotion, and he wasn't going back.

I want you to see that God had taken David through the training and development of his skill so that he was prepared for that day. David told King Saul, "I can do this. This is no problem because God has been with me, and He's with me now." Now, that was a mature seed; he responded as shrewdly as a snake. David knew he would take the giant out, so he gave his brothers the Happy Meals he brought to feed them and took up the challenge against the giant. David knew God was with him when He delivered him from the paw of the lion and the bear. David knew God would also deliver him from the hands of the Philistines. I want you to see that this is where you are. You are being trained in the situation you are in, and Jesus told me that I was to make sure that I told everyone that whatever battle you are in right now, whatever giant you will take out will be your promotion into your next level.

Your Soul Must Be in Sync with Your Spirit

When I was in junior high and high school, I ran every day, usually two miles. As I got a little older, I ran up to twenty miles a day, mostly once a week. I was so thin because I wanted to set many records, but then, I was beaten up by the bullies. I began lifting weights, and I became pretty big and muscular. Then I grew taller, but I still kept running. After that, everyone started to leave me alone except the guys who were threatened by my size and strength. Sometimes guys act just like a pack of wolves.

The biggest muscular guys in the school, the bullies, showed up because they wanted to challenge me to a fight, but I didn't want to fight. The head guy from school showed up one day at this triangle-shaped area where the roads met in my neighborhood. He had brought a bunch of guys with him to make sure I would fight him, so in reality, I was fighting four or five guys. As soon as this guy pulled his arm back to throw a punch at me, I went into a vision. I realized in that split second that I had already dreamed about this happening, so I knew exactly what he would do. I just moved my head and he missed, and I came up and knocked him out. I turned around and said, "Does anybody else want to die?" At that point, they all left, and I walked away, shaking. I said, "God, what just happened?" No one ever bothered me again after that.

God continued to give me dreams, including dreams about being on that road with those bullies. So I asked the Lord what was going on with this dream. When you have recurring dreams, you should ask the Holy Spirit about it because your spirit is trying to tell your soul something, but your soul is not up to speed yet. Your soul must be transformed, and you do that by renewing it in the Word of God. As you do, you will begin to synchronize with your spirit, and then your dreams will become clear. Essentially, your soul is an old Commodore 64, 8-bit computer, and your spirit is like some supercomputer, and they don't communicate properly. That same spirit that was attacking me through those guys wasn't able to get to me anymore, but that spirit was still after me.

One morning, I woke up at home in New Orleans before my wife was awake. I turned on the light on my nightstand and said "Yes" really loudly and began praying in tongues. Now my wife and I have this worked out. Whoever wakes up first says "Yes" loudly. This wakes up the other one, and then we both start praying in tongues, and that's how we start our day every morning. Now on this particular morning, when I began praying in tongues, I suddenly saw that triangle, that place in my old neighborhood where people wanted to fight me. Then I saw that I was no longer a victim, and it was flipped and the devil was the victim. This happened just a few years ago, and ever since that morning, I have never had that dream again. It all flipped around. So whatever is bothering or harassing you, it's a devil that is assigned to you, and you need to take them out because that's your assignment, and it will also be your ministry.

If you're thinking, *Could that really be true*? Remember what David ended up doing. He took out all the giants and trained thirty men to do exactly what he did with a slingshot. The devil you are to take out is bothering you, and that will be your promotion and your ministry. You need to take out whatever you're going through. I don't care if you're five years old or one-hundred-and-five years old. If you're still breathing, you can swing.

So, I ask you, what is bothering you? Maybe it's a traumatic event, and you don't understand why it happened, but you'll find out that God didn't have anything to do with it. When you get to heaven, you'll see at that moment that you weren't in a place where you could discern good and evil, so you didn't know how to discern or move and live and have your being fully in Him because if you did, you would have never found yourself in that situation. I want to train the body of Christ so we all get to that place now, here on the earth. I understand that some situations happen. This is a fallen world, and there are crazy people on earth.

The devils know when you mean business. They also know that you're called and chosen and that you are being prepared for something. They don't know the exact details, but they can see the activity. The devils know because you are lit up with the light of Christ. Even now, as you are reading the Word of God and about the Word, they see you're being visited because you light up in the Spirit.

When the breath of God comes upon you and when the Word of God ignites in you, all these different activities begin to happen. Angels come and stand beside you. Then the devils see all this activity, and then they reverse engineer; eventually, they will draw the conclusion that something's about to happen. They begin to fortify because they know they will be driven out because it will come to a point where your eyes in the Spirit start to see these entities. They will be found out, and then they can't operate. The Spirit of the Lord wants me to tell you that you will take your giant out, and God is preparing you with the tools you need.

CHAPTER 6

The Goodness of God

Do the riches of his extraordinary kindness make you
take him for granted and despise him? Haven't you
experienced how kind and understanding He has been to
you? Don't mistake his tolerance for acceptance. Do you
realize that all the wealth of his extravagant kindness is
meant to melt your heart and lead you into repentance?
—Romans 2:4 TPT

The heart of God is that everyone would repent and go to heaven. The truth is that God's ways are not our ways, and He knows exactly what a person needs for their heart to turn toward Him—an encounter with the goodness and love of the Father. When I was in heaven, I saw that everyone there wants every person to come to heaven, which is my heart too. I want to speak about the goodness of God so people are led to repentance and come into the rest of God.

God designed this wonderful salvation for everyone; however, the body of Christ has gotten off course and lost their edge along the way. But great news: I see that we are coming back even with the recent challenges we have faced. We're coming back just as when King David stepped into the position of kingship as he was anointed and appointed by God, and everyone quickly realized that there was a new sheriff in town. From that moment on, the situation started to change. King David developed his military, training the thirty fighting men, and before they knew it, he had a big army. King David boldly went after the giants, and when Israel went out to battle, they won. They became a world power at that time.

Hidden from Man but Not from God

God foreknew that Israel would require a change, and He had determined long before David became king that David would be the one to bring about those changes. Some may have seen David as a child, but many saw him as the most successful military conqueror in the history of Israel.

God trained David from a young boy, preparing him to become a king and mighty leader. Long before he was anointed as king, David sat under a tree playing his harp and doing target practice with his slingshot all day long. During this time, David had no idea that one day he would defeat the devil, but God made him ready. All the while, when David was just doing his thing out in the country, separate from the system, Jesus showed me that David picked targets. He practiced hitting whatever he could find: a tree, a bush, or a squirrel. That was how he became skilled with a slingshot, and we all know what he did with that slingshot.

During the earlier years in David's life, he may have been hidden from the world, but he was never hidden from God. God had His eye on David the entire time, using every situation in his life in preparation for the plans God had for him. This is like many of you, hidden from the world, but you're studying, praying, and doing the work of the Lord. You are obscure for now, but you're getting ready. You're building yourself up, praying in the Spirit, and developing your relationship with God. You're learning to hear His voice, and God is using you, maturing in the gifts so that you flow in the Spirit. You are creating relationships with people along the way, people that God is bringing into your life to build you up on your journey.

"Never despise what you may think are insignificant days."

For example, God used a person in my life that became my jet flight trainer. I flew with him for thirty years when I worked for Southwest Airlines. I saw him almost every day, and I had no idea that he would become my flight trainer one day. Now he flies down every month, and we go through six hours of training. Why? Because I'm getting ready. While he's training me, I do what I'm told, one step at a time. I've waited all my life for this, but if the Lord were to ask me to drop it, I would drop it. I don't care; I would buy a mountain bike instead if it meant obeying God.

But I developed a lifelong relationship with my trainer. I know that doesn't seem possible these days, but God can bring those types of people into your life, and you just know they will be with you for the long run. God did this as well with David and Jonathan. It almost seemed like an unlikely match since Jonathan was Saul's son, but you can see how God used this relationship to bless David.

When you look more closely at David's life, you can see how God was training him even when he had no idea how God was developing him. The point I want to make is never to despise what you may think are insignificant days. (See Zechariah 4:10.) They are not insignificant to God; as a matter of fact, it's just the opposite—they are significant as He is developing you and different relationships in your life.

Your Relationship with the Father Is Your Ministry

Making mistakes is part of learning. You are learning and growing, learning to work with people, learning how to flow with God. I make mistakes in my training; I have made mistakes every minute, but they start to lessen. You will make fewer and fewer mistakes as you grow and mature. You begin to understand and settle into your calling, and you transition into doing what works. You are in training, so you will make mistakes. God is developing you, and you're learning how to love Him and how to receive from Him. As He develops you, you begin to build confidence in your relationship with God, not from a place of pride. And from this place comes your ministry.

Jesus told me, "My relationship with My Father was My ministry." Now when have you ever heard that? This is the absolute truth; this is what Jesus did all the time. The Father was working through Him, and I don't think that we are any different. We can't just operate independently on our own.

David's Progression into God's Plan

Interestingly, as a young boy, David played his harp under the trees as he tended the sheep. I don't know; maybe the sheep sang along, saying *bah* in response to the music. During this time, David had no idea that he would be playing his harp, driving demons away from the former king of Israel one day. You can guarantee that was nowhere on his radar. He was not thinking about taking down a giant one day when he took down a lion and a bear. He was simply doing what a shepherd does and protecting the sheep. He didn't understand how anything he was doing was actually God training him for extraordinary things, but a day came when all things were made clear to him. It is the same for you. You may not see the big picture right now, but the day is coming when you will understand what's going on in your life. So while you are waiting for God to clarify these matters, just stay faithful with what you can do.

I went through a time in my life when God told me not to pursue piloting. I had gotten all the necessary ratings, and God told me to drop it, so I did. I dropped it for about twenty-five years; however, in the meantime, I built a small simulator in my home office, and I flew all the time. Well, I did crash a lot, but I flew a lot more. As time went on, the more I flew, the less I crashed. My wife sat with me in my office because she wasn't scared, and now she can sit with me on a real jet. When I look back on why Jesus told me not to pursue my pilot's training years ago, I now know that I wouldn't have had the time for what I'm doing now along with everything that would've been required. But like David, I knew that someday God would call my name and promote me, and I would get ready for it.

Your Preparation Will Cause a Manifestation

When I started my pilot training, the instructor said to me, "Man, I can see that you've been practicing."

So I asked him, "What are some areas where your other students are lagging behind?" As he would tell me what those areas were, I practiced those things repeatedly. Some of the areas he highlighted were taking off in flight as different issues were occurring, like losing an engine or having hydraulic problems. While in the simulator, at times, I'd practice losing both engines along with practicing all kinds of various scenarios. I would even create the scenario of flying in a thunderstorm where I wouldn't be able to land at the original, designated airport, which would force me to navigate a landing somewhere else, all while learning how to manage my fuel. This is an example of how you can prepare while God is in the process of training you. Whatever situation you find yourself in, ask yourself and pray with the mindset, "What can I be doing right now in the place where I find myself?"

After I had been to heaven, I wanted to start developing materials to teach from. At that time, I hadn't written any books yet, so I developed a study guide and a learning system that included Scriptures. I then asked if I could teach a Sunday School class. No one ever approached me asking me to teach or preach, but after I had been to heaven, I wanted to pour into the body anyway I could.

When I couldn't find a publisher to accept me, I became my own publisher. I bought a machine called a metal coil binder in the early days and made spiral notebooks. After continually bothering them about letting me teach a Sunday School class, they finally said yes. Everyone at the church happened to want to come to my class; eventually, they had to close it down because too many people were trying to fit into the room. Now I didn't understand what was happening at the time; all I knew was that I just wanted to get up there and teach.

When I was making and printing my study guides, I worked ten to fifteen hours on my days off, but see, this is how God develops you. Whatever you do, don't despise small beginnings. Always know that God is so good, and in that goodness, He can prepare you for something really big, which is what happened with David. During all the years God was preparing him, he was faithful in the way God led him. And when he reached the place where he played the harp for King Saul, David honored and served Saul because that's what God was leading him to do. God anointed David from the moment that Samuel anointed him, but in the process, he remained faithful for all those years, obeying God and following His lead and His timing.

Did you know that David did not become king for fifteen years from the day Samuel anointed him? He was just as anointed when he was a little kid and took out Goliath and when he had the thirty fighting men and won all those battles. This is precisely what's happening in the body of Christ right now. We are all anointed and we are all priests, and the way has been opened for us, so it's time to enter in and acknowledge that God is a good God.

Do Not Permit Fear to Paralyze You

Romans 8:28 says that God causes all things to work together for our good. How many things does it say will work together? It says *all things*. So no matter what's happening, He causes everything to work for your good. Even if you're getting hit, you have to keep moving because *He causes*. Jesus showed me that as you move, God starts to arrange the environment. So you have to keep moving; you can't stop or become paralyzed. Please promise me that you're listening.

You cannot allow fear to paralyze you. Many times, I have seen people becoming paralyzed with fear in various situations. Some of these people were in the same flight training class as me; they watched the same videos and did the same procedures. Yet I found out later that they died in an airplane crash because they didn't pull the handle for their parachute, or in an emergency, they ran.

When I worked for Southwest Airlines, I saw someone fall out with a heart attack a few times. I was waiting for the person who was supposed to be the lead step in, but they didn't. They went the other way, so I said, "Okay. Yes, I will do it." I then remembered my training, grabbed the oxygen and the CPR mask, and called the Med Link to call the hospital on the ground. I asked for a doctor to get on the phone right away, and I worked with them, and now they were in charge. Once we arrived at the nearest airport and a local doctor showed up, I'd look at their credentials, validating who they were, and I'd hand over the phone to them.

My point is, don't become paralyzed because someone's life—or even your own—might be at stake. In other words, you must train yourself so that no matter what, you will go into training mode; even if a gun barrel is pointed at you, you have to learn that the gun is not dangerous. The person that's holding it is dangerous, but only if he knows how to use it.

Demons can't handle someone that's not afraid because that's their only way of operating. A demon will get nervous when you're *not* nervous. I'm serious here; their only hope is that you don't know their mode of operation. They are cloaked so that you can't see them, and they will try to inject fear into you before they implement what they want to do. They try to brainwash and completely disarm you, both spiritually and physically. (This is what they did in Germany during WWII.)

The enemy wants to paralyze you so that you don't act appropriately, and then he just keeps escalating his attacks. David was promoted and did amazing feats with God, but we must remember that Romans 8:28 is saying that as you move forward, God is arranging your environment, causing all things to work together for good, not for the worse. If this is the case, then a lot of prophets would be fired because God causes all things to work together for good to those who love God. What does it mean to love God? It means that you obey His commands. There is no difference between love and obedience; they are the same. Jesus made that clear many times. People ask me questions about how long Jesus's hair was or the color of His eyes, but they don't ask me what He said. When you meet Him, you won't be able to answer any of those questions because you'll be flat on your face, so you won't remember the color of His eyes.

A Higher Level of Inheritance

As you keep moving, God *will cause*, which means He's influencing you, and you will begin seeing your high calling and destiny. As you go forward, you must stay diligent, not becoming lukewarm because we want to be found hot. After all, we want to spend most of our time in the throne room on the Sapphire Floor.

Jesus told me, "I didn't hang on a cross and go through what I went through for people to inherit the fence. I did it so that you can stand on the Sapphire Floor in the hottest spot in heaven." He then showed me all these Christians who had migrated to a fence, and one side represented the world, and the other side represented heaven. I was there with Him, and all the Christians were congregating around the long, stretched-out fence.

And He said, "My people are asking where the fence is so that they can live in the world and still go to heaven. They want to know where that spot is, where they'll just make it in." In other words, instead of asking where the hottest spot in heaven was, they wanted to know how close they could stand to the fence to do just enough to get to heaven.

And then He showed me places I would inherit all because I chose to walk in the fear of the Lord and in holiness and separation; in this, I inherited a place that He said most people would never know existed. Can you imagine spending eternity in heaven and not knowing there was more? He is a rewarder of those who diligently seek Him, and He will reward those who choose to sacrifice whatever it takes to walk with Him down here (Hebrews 11:6). Those people will receive the greater reward.

God Blesses Us with His Favor

"When you proclaim that God is good all the time, you are permitting Him to move on your behalf."

God once asked me to address and expose the sin of a church leader. It was not comfortable, but I did what God instructed me to do, regardless of the ramifications. Afterward, God said to me, "Because you stood up for me, I will stand up for you." Every day, I am reminded of that because He has given me favor. He's rewarding me even in this life because of what I did. Sadly, that leader lost everything, but when the Spirit leads you, God is involved in all the details, and He is causing everything to work out according to His good purpose. When you proclaim that God is good all the time, you are permitting Him to move on your behalf.

You Just Follow God's Lead

Before you take off for a flight, you put a flight plan together and enter it into the computer. Then the flight controller might change your departure and direct you to report to a different fix at a different altitude and a new location. Then you will need to change to another frequency and read it back to the controller to validate all the changes. These kinds of changes can really mess up your day because you had already set up navigation the way you wanted it, and it all changed in a minute.

What I found out is that no matter what, things change. I have learned that when I find myself in unknown situations or when I need to suddenly change my course, I must always stay in the joy of the Lord. What I go through is training, and I look for the good in everything God is doing.

This is true for everything in our lives; we must learn to move forward, recalculating along the way, knowing that change will happen. As you yield to the Spirit, He will speak to you and let you know the new plan because God will move you. When the course changes, the devil is tricked; he doesn't see the plan of God. It's like a chess game, and it's called warfare. The truth is that circumstances are not as set in stone as we think. The angels are very smart, and they are also directing you as they listen to their commander, Jesus. They have it all coordinated, and when the devil starts to move in a certain way, they have ways of tricking him. So you should pray in tongues all the time because you will then be praying through the Holy Spirit, who God gave to you as a Helper. He helps you pray perfect prayers, and then He answers them.

At times, God won't reveal everything to you up front. For example, He told Abraham to leave his home because God would take Abraham to a land that He would show him. But God didn't tell Abraham right away where He was leading him. Abraham asked, "God, where are we going?"

God said, "I'll show you when you get there. Just start walking in this direction." So sometimes, God might not give you the complete picture all at once. He may choose to lead you along the way as you go. But we can always have confidence that God knows where He's leading us and He knows the final destination even when we may not.

"We are hard pressed on every side, but not crushed; perplexed, but not in despair; persecuted, but not abandoned; struck down, but not destroyed. We always carry around in our body the death of Jesus, so that the life of Jesus may also be revealed in our body" (2 Corinthians 4:8–10 NIV). This verse says that we are hard-pressed on every side, and I know we all feel that at times. I tell my wife sometimes that I can feel the breath of the dragon down the back of my neck. When that happens, I keep moving because God is causing me to triumph. I do not allow what is happening to influence my emotions or the direction of my thoughts. I consider not these things because they are light and momentary, and I know that circumstances change. When I grew up in Pennsylvania, people used to say, "If you don't like the weather, just wait two hours. It'll change."

When you encounter resistance, it may be because you're doing the right thing. When I feel resistance, I can still speak the same message, and I might feel bad the whole time I'm speaking, but I know that the angels are fighting for me and that I will reach the place where resistance is gone. This is why it's so vital to keep following God, staying the course, and staying close to the Spirit because He will lead and guide you through any resistance. If you find yourself off track at any time, get back on course immediately!

God Gives Provision for Your Vision

Jesus told me a secret that I've never heard anyone else say. He said, "Kevin, before we give a person a vision, we actually provide for that vision ahead of time, and it's called provision. We then reveal the vision to the person." So when a person receives a vision of what God wants to do for them or through them, the person may immediately think, *How will I pay for this*? But God is good all the time, and He has already provided what you will need before He ever gives you the vision. The provision has already been earmarked. Someone else may have your money, but you can rest assured it has already been set aside for you.

Be Sober-Minded

Likewise, exhort the young men to be sober-minded, in all things showing yourself to be a pattern of good works; in doctrine showing integrity, reverence, incorruptibility, sound speech that cannot be condemned, that one who is an opponent may be ashamed, having nothing evil to say of you" (Titus 2:6). To be prepared for when God shifts things, we need to be sober-minded and discerning. If we get off track or lose focus, then suddenly, when the season changes, we might think, "Whoa, when did this happen?" But as you are showing yourself faithful in good works and doctrine, showing integrity, reverence, and incorruptibility, you will stay on the course, knowing that God is good, and He will lead you into His purposes for you.

God may lead you into something that you never saw coming, like when He told us to start our own network. I knew that it would be very expensive, but this is what can happen. It may be costly or inconvenient, and some people might say, "Why are you doing this?"

But isn't that what they said to Noah? And we know how that turned out. Noah got all the animals on the ark, along with his family, and then he reached out the window and put an LED sign on the outside, saying No Vacancy. But see, people had time to repent, and God also sent prophets who were telling them of the impending doom. Enoch himself warned the people of the judgment to come, and after he received the word from the Lord, he named his son Methuselah, which meant "death shall bring" as a prophetic sign. His son Methuselah lived to be 969 years old, and he died a year before the flood.

We Move Up in the Spirit by Revelation

God meant it when He told us to "come out from among them and be separate, do not touch what is unclean, and I will receive you" (2 Corinthians 2:17). Yes, God is good, but He has given us clear instructions. I am telling you to be sure that you have separated yourself from this world because a time will come when it's too late. You will be snagged. How do you separate yourself? You start first with your heart; then the Spirit will instruct you on what to do because you come out from the world through revelation. That is how we pull rank. The enemy cannot move by revelation. When God gives you a word, it is powerful and undefeatable unless you back off. When you move by revelation, you go into the Spirit.

> *"We were all created in God's image;*
> *we are designed to move by revelation."*

Jesus commended Peter when he said, "Thou art the Christ, the son of the living God" (Matthew 16:16 KJV). And in verse 17, Jesus praised him, saying, "Blessed are you for flesh and blood is not revealed this to you but my Father, which is in Heaven." The church was built on this revelation—the revelation of Jesus Christ. The gates of hell will not prevail against the church because of this. We were all created in God's image; we are designed to move by revelation.

Being Confident of Your Victory

With confidence, you should remind yourself every day that you're going somewhere and that you're being trained, being promoted, and you will be ready whenever the occasion arises. Practice your CPR because you might need to use it one day, and you might save our next president. You might save a prophet or a prophetess. If you are a paramedic or work in a hospital, you might treat someone who is a mouthpiece for God. You must know that everything is planned. We all fall into it, and events might seem random, but when you get to heaven, you will see that they weren't random at all. Some people ask, "What is my purpose?" Well, even asking that question is a good sign, but the thing is, you are fulfilling your purpose with every breath you take. Why? Because you're moving and living. Satan wants to stop you, but God wants you to keep going because He sees what He wrote for you.

Second Timothy 3:12 says, "Yes, and all those who desire to live godly in Christ Jesus will suffer persecution." Once you start moving in the direction God is leading you, the persecution will begin, and it's actually spiritual. Just know it will manifest through people, those who yield to the enemy. Isn't that what Paul told us, that we do not wrestle with flesh and blood (Ephesians 6:12)? I'm telling you this because you need to know that you cannot take it personally when you are doing things right, and then something wrong happens. Remembering that if you encounter resistance, it doesn't mean you've done something wrong. Persecution manifests first in the spirit.

A demon doesn't always have access to people, but when they find those people they can access, they pursue them, and then the manifestation occurs. Before manifestation, persecution is an invisible war around you. If you get close to someone who is a numbskull, you will watch them start to fold before your eyes and become a Peter popping off with their words. For example, he told Jesus that He wouldn't go to Jerusalem to die. Jesus had to explain that He knew where He was going and that Peter was not speaking from the right spirit. Jesus was doing warfare. We are to pull down any stronghold that exalts itself against the knowledge of God (2 Corinthians 10:4–5). This is what you do. Peter allowed a spirit that was exalting itself above what was already known as the will of God to speak through him, and Jesus had to pull it down. It didn't matter where the words were coming from; they had to be pulled down.

When I died and was with Jesus, separate from my body, I saw that the veil of the flesh and the soul was obscuring the beauty of who I really was in the spirit. From that time on, I had to be diligent down here in order to walk in the spirit.

That walk would not just come naturally. I had to be diligent to pray, meditate on the Word of God, and not to listen to people with the Peter syndrome because they can slant you in a certain direction, and before you know it, you're way off track, thinking, *How did this happen?* Satan operates one step at a time and one voice at a time. The demon spirits will find the weakest link in your family, your friends, or your government, and they will try to deteriorate you. I have had to shut those voices off, and you're my family, so I want you to know this too.

God Wants You to Expect Payback

"Blessed are you when men hate you, and when they exclude you, and revile you, and cast your name as evil, for the Son of Man's sake. Rejoice in that day and leap for joy! For indeed your reward is great in heaven, for in like manner their Fathers did to the prophets" (Luke 6:22–23). God is good, and He's given us His Word so that we understand what we are dealing with when persecution comes. You will go through suffering for His sake, but the price you pay is not as great as the reward that comes because God will make sure that you can see God's normal in how He rewarded Jesus. Jesus pointed out to me that after He was tempted in the desert, angels came and tended to Him (Matthew 4:11). So He had an angelic visitation, right? I am pleading with you because my Father in heaven is pleading through me to you. Please believe for an angelic encounter after you have been tempted because they want to minister to you. God wants you to know that you should expect payback when you go through temptations and trials.

Your Life Is an Advertisement of God's Power

Romans 2:4 says, "Or do you despise the riches of His goodness, forbearance, and long-suffering, not knowing that the goodness of God leads you to repentance?" This is a refrigerator verse. He draws people to Himself through the manifestation of His goodness and love because it's His will that no one perishes. So Paul asked, "Do you despise the riches of His goodness?" I don't even know if I'm allowed to say that in church. The revelation of God's goodness changed Moses to the point that people saw it in his face, which was shining so brightly when he came down from that mountain that the people were afraid of him (Exodus 34:30). This change came about when God told Moses, "I will make all my goodness pass before you" (Exodus 33:19). Did you know that after Moses experienced God's goodness, he couldn't die because he had been with God? God had to actually pronounce his death, or he would have just kept on living. Moses died at 120 years of age, and his eyesight was not failing, and his body was strong; he was full of strength (Deuteronomy 34). Why? Because he spent all that time with God, becoming a friend of God to the point it transformed his body.

Ephesians 1:19–21 (TPT) says, "I pray that you will continually experience the immeasurable greatness of God's power that's made available to you through faith. Then your lives will be an advertisement of this immense power as it works through you!" The same mighty power that was released when Jesus was raised from the dead is the advertisement coming through you. Your life is full of immense power, which is the advertisement that others will see. God then exalted Jesus to the highest place of honor and supreme authority in heaven. That same power that rose Jesus from the dead and put Him on the throne is within us.

God's Success Transferred to the Next Generation

God's plan is for no division in the body of Christ. The body can't be divided and still function as one. It can only function as one within God's design, with the head as Jesus Himself, and us prepared as His bride. The preparer is a good God, the Father of all. He sent the Holy Spirit, who is training and preparing us. He has anointed and appointed the fivefold to build us up in unity. This is what Jesus did; Jesus didn't separate Himself apart from the people and say, "I'm the Son of God, and that's why I can do these miracles." No, He said, "You will do the same thing" (John 14:12). He wouldn't let people call Him the Son of God. He wanted to be called the Son of Man because He wanted to be equal with man. He left the glory and left His heavenly Father to be with us. Philippians 2:7 says that Jesus "made Himself of no reputation, taking the form of a bondservant and coming in the likeness of men." He considered equality with God as nothing and chose to come as a man. Jesus wanted to replicate Himself.

Jesus wanted the disciples to replicate Him, and then He wanted them to exceed Him (John 14:12). See, this is what a good God does; He wants to transfer His success to the next generation, and the next and the next. It's like with a corporation or a non-profit. You groom someone to take over so that the person has your exact vision and heart, and you put a whole board of lawyers in place to make sure they do it. I'm encouraging you now. When an angel comes, he has been to the throne room, and he has beheld the face of your Father. When he comes back and stands with you, he brings heaven with him, and he's energized from just being in God's presence. They come back in full force and stand beside you. They watch you and respond to God's presence. Within that presence, you don't understand this, but you will.

When that angel is standing there, you are in the perfect will of God because he is in the perfect will of God by association. You might be messed up, but it won't take long if you begin to yield to Him and acknowledge that He is a good God and that this angel has been sent to help you and minister to you. As the angel ministers to you, you will feel God's freedom because that angel has been instructed in a special assignment to make sure that you don't even trip. I want you to be encouraged and validated that you are doing better than you think. As you yield to the Holy Spirit and the angels that are sent to help you, you'll begin to see circumstances working out for your good. Remember another secret: When God chooses you, He's not choosing you based on your ability but based on your availability and because of your heart. God knows He can work with you.

CHAPTER 7

Children of God

But as many as received Him, to them He gave the right
to become children of God.

—John 1:12

This verse explains how our relationship with Jesus begins. We become children of God when we receive Him. You can say that Jesus is our brother as well, right? Doesn't He say, I call you brothers, sisters, and friends, not servants (Hebrews 2:11; John 15:15)? See, it's all about relationship. Now I want you to hear me out and put this on your refrigerator. The religious system will never allow you to let Jesus be your brother, and they will never let you be His friend. In John 8:25, the Pharisees asked Jesus, "Who are you?" The reason they said this was because they had placed themselves in a position of importance to control the people, and they had a big money-making scheme going on. The entire system was rigged against the people because they placed pressure on people, making them feel guilty for their sins. They kept the people on edge so they would always need someone. Does this sound familiar to you? When you are a child of God, you can go directly to your heavenly Father yourself, but the religious system doesn't want you to do that. You know that you can go to your Daddy yourself, right? You don't have to go through anyone to reach Him.

"As children, we inherit the same vision that God has, and then we promote it wherever we go."

The fivefold ministry is not here to control you. God has established them to cheer you on. It's the government of God, and He is a good God because everything about Him is good, including His people. We don't need to steal, manipulate, or control people. We are free, but we must protect that freedom and adopt the vision of our heavenly Father. Jesus said, "Did you not know that I must be about my Father's business?" (Luke 2:49). So God is a businessman. Why else would He use that word there? Jesus had the vision of His Father, and He was promoting His Father's business because He would inherit it. As children, we inherit the same vision that God has, and then we promote it wherever we go.

"And if children, then heirs—heirs of God and joint-heirs with Christ, if indeed we suffer with Him, that we may also be glorified together" (Romans 8:17). Because we represent God, we are coheirs, and since we are coheirs, we get the business too. That's how powerful this is. We know that we have been adopted as children of God, and along with that, we have taken the name of God as our name. Everyone should relate to us as associated with God. The people and Jewish leaders identified that the disciples had been with Jesus because they were acting like Him, and the same things that had happened with Jesus were happening with them. It is not as common to see miracles today, but it should be.

The only way to build your faith is by the revelation of the Word of God, and you have to hear it because your faith does come by hearing, and it has double the impact when spoken—it is a continual or a perpetual action. The English language does not have a way to emphasize a repeated word, but the Aramaic uses "Surely, surely." Other times, when Jesus repeated a word, He meant that the word is being continued. For example, Ephesians 5:18 says to be filled, and it means to be "continuously filled." It's continual and perpetual. It starts, and it should never slow down, and it should never diminish at all.

Each one of us should have a daily testimony about what God has done for us because it's the evidence to others that He's with us and will manifest because we are His children. It is a testimony that we have His name in and on us, and the angels have been assigned to us. Now that's supernatural, and it means that everything we do is blessed. We shouldn't have any curses working in our lives.

Whenever something is not manifesting and I know it is my inheritance, I don't just keep doing things the same way; I will automatically go to God and say, "Obviously, nothing is wrong with you, so there's only one other party here, and it's me." I turn myself in all the time. I continually stay humble and weak. I am constantly accountable and acknowledge that I don't know everything; that way, God is always gracious with me, and because I keep my heart in this posture, He speaks to me even in my weakness and ignorance. He will always do this for you too.

> *"God is preemptive and preventative, and that's who we have a relationship with."*

If you want to undermine what the enemy is doing, you have to be a couple of steps ahead of him. However, if you look at past presidential administrations, for example, they would say, "Well, we'll fix it when it breaks." But it was already broken. That's the world's mentality; they won't fix something until they have to. But see, if you are on a flight and something broke down while you were in mid-air, you definitely wouldn't want the mechanic to tell you that. No, you would expect them to operate in a preventive manner, right?

God is preemptive and preventative, and that's who we have a relationship with as His children. We have intimate details. Jesus said, "I do not call you servants any longer, for the servant does not know what his master is doing, but I have called you [My] friends because I have revealed to you everything that I have heard from My Father" (John 15:15 AMP). A servant doesn't have intimate knowledge of what the master is doing, but the master's friends do. Jesus has given us the ability to receive from Him through the Spirit of God and the Word of God; we have intimate details and understanding about His vision and what He wants.

We Are All the Sons of God

Some of us haven't experienced a father's love because of this fallen world. Before my dad passed away, he called me in tears, repenting to me, and he told me, "You're helping so many people. Do you have any idea what you are doing in this world? Just keep doing what you're doing." My dad became my biggest fan. He used to call me every week, and I saw that he was broken.

The last time I spoke to him, he told me that he became a Christian because he saw God manifest in my life. After that, he went into a coma and died, but I can hear him yelling from heaven at the top of his lungs right now. He's yelling for me to keep going. "Tell them more." Why was my dad my biggest fan? Because he saw Jesus in me, which convinced him to become a Christian. That is the biggest thing you can do for God. Let Him shine through you, and you be the light in the world.

To be a light, we have to discuss controversial topics. No one will go there, so I will. Romans 8:19 says, "For the earnest expectation of the creation eagerly waits for the revealing of the sons of God." Some people will be offended by the use of the word "sons" here, but did you know that wherever the word "son" is written, it's really the word for "children?" Another discrepancy is regarding the written Hebrew word used for "God," which is *Elohim*, a plural word. In Hebrew, it is improper to have a singular noun but write it as a plural. There is only one God, but His name is represented as plural. The correct spelling of the singular noun would be *Eloah*. This is important because the Hebrew word *Elohim* is technically inaccurate; however, it represents the Trinity. Many Christians know the truth about the triune God— Father, Son, and Holy Spirit—but some do not have a clear understanding about this, which is why the translation of God's name can be so controversial.

Interestingly, we also have masculine descriptors. We are made in the image of God, male and female, but the female came out of the man. Adam was created first, and then the female came out of him. In heaven, we are neither male nor female, and Jesus said that there would be no marriage or gender (Luke 20:34; Galatians 3:28). Thank God, no one is sexually confused in heaven. On earth, there is confusion because of the flesh, but in heaven, there is none, and we are all the sons of God.

A curse was on Adam, Eve, the serpent, and on the land. The reason that God pronounced the curse on each one was that each one is individually different. In heaven, we are all one, and by the Spirit of God, we are made one here on earth.

Positional versus Relational Access

"And these signs will follow those who believe: In My name they will cast out demons; they will speak with new tongues; they will take up serpents; and if they drink anything deadly, it will by no means hurt them; they will lay hands on the sick, and they will recover" (Matthew 16:17–18). God established the church, the body of Christ, and according to Jesus, the gates of hell would not prevail against it (Matthew 16:18). We are the believing ones, the *ecclesia*, and as a result, signs will follow those who believe—in other words, us. It does not say, "Signs will follow the fivefold." We must understand this because we're getting off track in this area. We are not to wait for an apostle to come into town to hear from God or get a word from him. You can look in the mirror and tell yourself to repent. You can give yourself a word each day, and you can wage war with the prophecies you have already received.

At one time, I thought I had access to certain things in heaven, and Jesus made me aware that I did not. At a particular spot in heaven, Jesus put His hand out, stopped me, and said, "You can't come in unless I bid you come." I then realized I had wrong thinking in some areas. We've been taught that we have access to all these benefits through Jesus Christ; however, Jesus taught me that we do have access to everything positionally through Him, but some things require a relationship to gain access. See, there is a difference between positional and relational.

Through the shed blood and the completed work on the cross, Jesus Christ gave us the ability to go into the holy of holies. He also made us righteous and holy, positionally. However, we can also see the faith of Abraham and the establishment of friendship through relationship. He was also called the friend of God. David and Moses both had a friendship with God. Through a friendship with God, we can understand the idea of a relationship with Him. In Matthew 7:22, Jesus says, "Many will say to Me in that day, 'Lord, Lord, have we not cast out demons in Your name, and done many wonders in your name?' And then I will declare to them, 'I never knew you; depart from Me, you who practice lawlessness.'"

What does it mean to know someone? Doesn't knowing someone suggest that you have a relationship with them? For example, you can work for a company, but you may not have a relationship with the company's president. Even though the company hired you, the president may not even know who you are. However, if you know the CEO, you would have more than just a position. You would have a relationship.

If you saw suspicious activity or witnessed a crime, you would be sure to report the problem to the local police, right? In the same way, we are called to steward God's vision and to be His ambassadors. You are God's eyes on this earth; you are the watchman. You are His eyes and ears, and He will give you abilities above and beyond because you are His children. As children of God, we receive the briefings from our heavenly Father. We are not supposed to be kept out of

His inside revelation. We are supposed to have all understanding. We are down here in this realm because God trusts us, and we want justice and righteousness to reign in this nation and for the people of this country.

As God's Children, We Have the Answers

The time is now for the church to stand up, and I can see we are already standing. I could spend a week talking about the things I've seen, and it would shock you but it shouldn't. Now I know that we, as the children of God, have the answers to the problems. We are the answer and the solution to the challenges. We have the keys to help someone, and we all have something that we can offer. I'm telling you all this because now is the time for people to be validated and informed about who they are; the Spirit of God wants to validate people, but He has to overcome their will first. Jesus told me that He shouldn't have to overcome someone's will; instead, we should be cooperating with Him. He shouldn't have to mention some things because we should just already know them.

"That you may be blameless and harmless, the sons of God without rebuke amid a crooked and perverse generation, among whom you shine as lights in the world" (Philippians 2:15). We need the Word of God being preached. We need to call it as it is and be straightforward. If all you have is a feel-good message every Sunday, you won't have to have this sharpness. We won't have a sharp sword if the Word of God is not being preached. This verse in Philippians is saying that we remain blameless and harmless, as the sons of God without rebuke, even though we live in a perverse generation. This means that God doesn't have to rebuke us. You have to remember this because it's reality, and it means that righteousness will reign. God never dies, He never ceases, and He doesn't diminish, and so we know that He is gaining territory. He's not giving up any ground, and we're not supposed to either.

A Better Covenant

"So, God has given both his promise and his oath. These two things are unchangeable because it is impossible for God to lie. Therefore, we who have fled to him for refuge can have great confidence as we hold to the hope that lies before us" (Romans 8:18). Some prophets today will speak out of their own imagination, which means that they are not interpreting or speaking the true gospel message. You will hear messages saying that God's children are appointed to wrath; are you kidding me? Look at the Israelite slaves; they were not judged by the plagues of Egypt, were they? Egypt is a representation of the world. Now, think about it; this was the Old Testament. What do you think the New Testament is? Isn't it based on even better promises and a better covenant (Hebrews 8:16–18)? I don't know about you, but I'm feeling that better covenant right now. I'm feeling the goodness of God.

"But this is that which was spoken by the prophet Joel; and it shall come to pass in the last days, saith God, I will pour out of my Spirit upon all flesh: and your sons and your daughters shall prophesy, and your young men shall see visions, and your old men shall dream dreams" (Acts 2:16–17). Now, do you think that the blood from a lamb that the Israelites placed above their doorpost is more effective than the blood of Jesus? I want the pure message of the gospel preached in all the world. Either we are forgiven, kept pure, and protected, or we're not. And if I'm not, I'm getting out, and I'll find something else. But we know that this *is* that— "that which was spoken by the prophet Joel." And it was spoken by all the prophets, not just Joel.

Be Careful Not to Become Disqualified

In heaven, I saw something I can't say on talk shows. I have produced my own talk show so that I can talk about what I've seen. I saw that without demon spirits on the earth, a Christian would not sin simply because they were removed. If this were so, you could deal with your flesh. You wouldn't believe the difference it would make. As a result of the presence of evil and the influence of demons around us, working on us constantly, we are pulled away by our own desires. If we didn't have demons to seduce us, we could keep our desires in check because they wouldn't be as strong. Now, you still have no excuse because you do have a will, but I also saw how strong we were. If a demon were not allowed to come near you, you would have enough influence from the Holy Spirit to do the right thing, and you would gravitate more freely toward righteousness because that's already in you, in your spirit. Inwardly, you are holy and righteous.

Paul understood the devil's influence on our flesh; he said that after preaching Christ, if he didn't discipline his body, he could be a castaway and become disqualified from the race because his body would rule him (1 Corinthians 9:27).

This is why he called the Corinthians "carnal" even though they were spiritual people. They were demonstrating the gifts everywhere, but at the same time, they were also carnal. Paul told the church of Corinth to stop drinking milk and start eating meat and move on as mature Christians. How should they do that? By disciplining their flesh.

Preparation for the Next Move

A time will come when evil will be taken away. We will have a thousand-year reign. We will be down here on the earth, and people will be populating the world, but satan will not be present because he will be bound for those thousand year (Revelation 20). This has nothing to do with Armageddon or the bowls of wrath. We are being prepared right now for those thousand years, which is why I want to teach you so that you will be ready for it. As children of God, we will rule and reign in the new city of Israel. The city will come down from heaven and will be set within the boundaries where the entire Middle East is now. The actual size will be fifteen hundred miles, and the borders will be those that are recorded in Genesis, the original size that God planned. It is not supposed to be the size of New Jersey like it is now.

Some vile people will be outside the city walls (Revelation 22:15). Satan will not be present because he will be locked up. And I saw where we could come in and out of the city, and they would not be able to touch us. We will be ruling and reigning with Him for a thousand years. We will be ambassadors and will be over countries and cities, taking care of God's kingdom. At the end of that time, satan will be loosed for a short time to tempt people. After that, another process will occur, but I don't understand what will happen with those people. Then again, it doesn't fit into the end-time charts.

So everyone will need to redo their DVDs and their prophecy charts because I won't be sitting around on a cloud eating grapes. I will be walking around, ruling and reigning over certain territories that have been assigned to me, and so will you. We will be the sons of God, and they won't be able to touch us.

The Lord asked me to share this with you because He wants you to know what we are being prepared for, and you need to know that it's just starting. We are waiting for one thing to happen, and then we think we'll get to live in our mansions. Your mansion is there, just as Jesus said it would be. Can you see now why I'm frustrated? It's because the body of Christ is supposed to realize who they are and call all the shots.

If you were to talk to the new agers, socialists, satanists, or any of the parties with an ungodly agenda, they would tell you that they believe Christians and churches hold everyone back. They know they can't control the church, and now they don't want the church to meet or sing. But we will meet and sing. We will love each other and get closer. Why? Because we are looking at what's ahead and getting ready.

During this final move on the earth, the church is supposed to have a voice and have the characteristics of our heavenly Father. God gave us our voice because we are to have one, and we are to use it. Those who are opposed to God and His righteousness want to cover our mouths. They don't want to allow us to communicate, and they don't want us to be close to one another. At the tower of Babel, God said that nothing man imagined would be impossible for them when they came together, and God had to separate them because their hearts were bent on evil.

*"Since we speak the same language
in the Spirit, we are one."*

Since Pentecost, we are now in unity in the Spirit, which is a miracle. What God said hasn't changed; it's still the same. When we come together, nothing shall be impossible for us, but God's not worried about that now. Why? Because our hearts are bent on good, not evil. What happened at Babel was reversed on the day of Pentecost. Since we speak the same language in the Spirit, we are one. That should bring revelation as to why Jesus said, "Again I say to you that if two of you agree on earth concerning anything that they ask, it will be done for them by My Father in heaven" (Matthew 18:19). Do you get it? Doesn't the media also know that if we agree as touching any one thing when our hearts are bent on good, we will get what we've asked for?

We Are Anointed and Appointed

As children of God, we have been appointed, and we are anointed, which means we have been set apart for a purpose. With that anointing comes a yolk-breaking ability. Jesus didn't just talk about His anointing; He demonstrated it. Everywhere Jesus went, He told people that He would not be with them much longer and that they needed to get this. And He told them that they would do greater works than Him (John 14:12). The religious system will not allow you to relate to Jesus in that way. To do that, they said, "Okay, what we'll do is we'll just say that when the apostles died, so did that commission. We don't need tongues anymore because that was just to get the church started." This system tried to tell me that I did not need tongues and that they were the authority. I want to know who gave them the authority because I don't see their names in the Bible.

You won't be in a religious system because they will not let you recognize yourself as a child of God, and they certainly won't confirm that you can do the things that the apostles or even the early believers did. But who gave them the authority to do that? A lot of councils met to determine these things. I've read the minutes from those councils, and it shows they were arguing at one of those meetings because some people initially said that the books of Jude and James shouldn't be in the Bible. Can you believe that? Jude and James didn't make it on the first round. It's a good thing I wasn't in that meeting because I need Jude and James. When you think about it, satan didn't want the book of Jude in there because it mentions Enoch.

You would also find the book of Jasher mentioned at least four times in those minutes. Jasher was mentioned in the Bible as well (Joshua 10:13; 2 Samuel 1:18; 2 Timothy 3:8). The book of Jasher didn't make it in the canon of Scripture, but we can reference this historical book. My point is, these people were determining what was going in the Bible and what was not, and you can read how they argued about it. You can even read about a disagreement where they were trying to determine how many angels could fit onto the head of a pin. I'm not kidding you. You must ask yourself whether we really want these guys deciding if Jude would make it in the Bible. I went to Bible School, and it actually hurt me for a while because I learned about subjects that I probably didn't need to know as a young Christian. However, now I'm glad I did learn those things because I'll depend on the Bible and on the Holy Spirit. If we do that, we have more than enough.

The Children of God Finish in the Spirit

Paul was so angry at the Galatians when he said, "Are you going to finish in the flesh what you started in the spirit?" (Galatians 3:3). He was essentially asking, "Who moved in and broke your stride?" Paul told them they were bewitched, which means that a curse had been put on them by a witch. In Revelation 2:4, Jesus said, "I have this against you, that you have left your first love." Jesus warned those seven churches in Turkey, and they're all gone now. Jesus was saying here to return to your first love so we can all move on to the next stage. You can see how we can get off course and how we need to follow the Spirit, remembering that eventually, the religious system will fully merge with the antichrist government.

Some supposedly Christian leaders seem to think that there are many ways to God. But Jesus said, "I am the way the truth and the life and no one comes to the Father except by me" (John 14:6). They also think that Christians need to stop evangelizing and making people feel uncomfortable. I want to know if they want to take the hit when their followers end up in hell. Do you want to take the responsibility for that because you're telling Christians not to warn people of the coming wrath so they can be saved? The religious system allows leaders to misuse their authority. If you have a true church with a true pastor who preaches the true gospel, I encourage you to help him, pray for him, and attend as much as possible because church is fun. It isn't fun anymore when you feel manipulated and controlled. When that happens, I would rather say, can I just send in my money? Because, in the end, that's what this kind of establishment is really about. Why are churches not prospering? It's because they don't believe in it.

Supernatural Provision for God's Children

Years ago, Kathi and I asked how we would do it if we ever went into ministry. In the prosperity of heaven's kingdom, you should have plenty of money to do whatever you want for the kingdom and not be under pressure or compulsion to give. You should be prosperous to the point that the churches are the most prosperous institutions. Jesus never said that they would have to shut down. No, when the money bag became low in funds, Peter just said, "Let's go catch some fish," and Jesus filled His boat with fish. Why? Because Jesus took care of His boys, His fellow ministers.

When the temple tax collectors came to Peter and said, "Does your teacher not pay the temple tax?" Peter explained that Jesus did make payments. When he arrived where Jesus was, Jesus already knew what the tax collectors had asked, so He asked Peter, "From whom do the kings of the earth collect duty and taxes—from their own children or from others?" Peter explained that they collected taxes from others. So Jesus said to him, "Then the children are exempt, But so that we may not cause offense, go to the lake and throw out your line. Take the first fish you catch; open its mouth and you will find a four-drachma coin. Take it and give it to them for my tax and yours" (Matthew 17:26–27 NIV).

This coin must have been enough money to pay Jesus's taxes for a few years. But what was Jesus doing here? Didn't he say that the sons of the kingdom are exempt but to pay taxes so that we don't offend them? And this is because He's from another kingdom, but Jesus honored the government here, and God also provided supernaturally for it. I share more about this in my book, *Supernatural Finances*, explaining in more detail how it's not about giving. It's about the truth that supernatural finances are for His children; it is God's normal for us.

God Reveals His Strategy to His Children

When David faced a battle, he always waited and sought God. The army sat there, cleaning and sharpening their swords, ready to go. You know, "lock and load." David then said, "No, hold on. I need to inquire of the Lord." He put on the ephod and asked God, "Shall we go up against them? Will you give them into our hands or not?"

He asked the Lord, and the Lord answered, "Go, I've given them to you." God then gave David a battle strategy. Because of this, all the surrounding nations knew not to mess with Israel.

A Christian who is legitimately walking with God will have fruit and the power of God in their life. We must understand that all the blessings given to Abraham in the Old Testament are on us individually as heirs of God because we are children of Abraham (Galatians 3:29). Through faith, we have been grafted in, and now we have the blessings of Abraham (Romans 11:17). So what was the blessing of Abraham? Even though Abraham had departed from his country, leaving everything behind, the Bible says he was very rich (Genesis 12–13). So how did he become very rich?

Because God blessed him and his son, Isaac. Isaac sowed in famine and reaped a hundred-fold (Genesis 26:12). See, God was displaying to the nations, through Isaac, that He was his God.

Partakers of His Divine Nature

"By which have been given to us exceedingly great and precious promises, that through these you may be partakers of the divine nature, having escaped the corruption that is in the world through lust" (2 Peter 1:4). Peter said that we are a partaker, a partner, with God in His divine nature. This means that you will see God's normal become your normal, which will be very abnormal to everyone else, especially with people who have an agenda that is opposite of God's. Those people will have agendas and see Christians as being in the way.

There is therefore no condemnation to those who are in Christ Jesus, who do not walk according to the flesh, but according to the spirit. For the law of the Spirit of life in Christ Jesus has made us free from the law of sin and death. For what the law could not do in that it was weak through the flesh, God did by sending His own Son in the likeness of sinful flesh, on account of sin: He condemned sin in the flesh, that the righteous requirement of the law might be fulfilled in us who do not walk according to the flesh but according to the Spirit. (Romans 8:1–4)

The flesh made the law weak, meaning we couldn't keep the law. God did something so amazing when He sent His own Son. Jesus wasn't sent in the likeness of God the Father— no. He sent His Son in the likeness of sinful flesh, and the Scripture says that the righteous requirement of the law was fulfilled. Jesus is sitting on a throne because He succeeded in fulfilling it. Therefore now, we do not walk according to the flesh but according to the Spirit. This means life is in your spirit. When Peter says that everything you need for life and godliness has been deposited in you, this means you already have it (2 Peter 1:3). You don't have to buy a DVD series to get it. It's already there inside you.

Rest Set Aside for God's Children

As God's children, did you know that we honor Him with a day of rest? "Remember that you were a slave in the land of Egypt, and the Lord, your God, brought you out from there by a mighty hand and an outstretched arm. Therefore, the Lord, your God commanded you to keep the Sabbath day" (Deuteronomy 5:15). Also, Hebrews 4:1 says, "Therefore, since the promise of entering his rest still stands, let us be careful that none of you be found to have fallen short of it." As children of God, we honor God one day each week so that we don't kill ourselves. "Let us, therefore, make every effort to enter that rest, so that no one will perish by following their example of disobedience" (Hebrews 4:11 NIV). And so, we enter into the promises of God and into the rest, but we also keep the Sabbath. We have one day of rest so that we can fulfill our lives down here. If you follow God's commands regarding this, it will go better with you, and you will live longer. In Mark 2:27, Jesus said, "The Sabbath was made for man, and not man for the Sabbath." The Sabbath was made to help man.

In the same way, God didn't think, "Hey, we'll make a tithe and then create man so that he'll tithe." God isn't trying to get something from you; He wants *all* of you. God is trying to help you, and this is how He does it. If you do certain things while on earth, you will live a lot longer, and you will have abundance, and life will go well for you. If God were really in control, He would force you to tithe and keep the

Sabbath. But He doesn't do that because you can do what you want. I have to tell you, that scares me; God lets us do what we want. God always wants what is best for His children because He only has a good plan for our lives.

CHAPTER 8

Times and Seasons

And the children of Issachar, who were men

who had an understanding of the times, to know

what Israel ought to do.

—1 Chronicles 12:32

G od establishes the times and the seasons. As the body of Christ, we have entered into another season. When Jesus told the disciples not to depart from Jerusalem but to wait for the promise of the Father, the disciples asked Him, "Lord, will You at this time restore the kingdom to Israel?" In reply, Jesus said to them, "It is not for you to know times or seasons which the Father has put in His own authority" (Acts 1:6–7). When God determines that it is time for man to know what He is doing, He makes it known to the prophets beforehand (Amos 3:7).

God tells me the times and locations that He wants me to schedule meetings because he has planned to release specific things through me for the people who will be there or those who will be hearing the message online. I have experienced God's plan for me to be around certain leaders so I would receive a transfer of their anointing or an impartation of what they carry to support what He is doing in that season in my life. God sets up connections with specific people at specific times in all our lives to come along and support and lift us up exactly when we need it. God knows what is required to bring about His plan, and He establishes the times and seasons to accomplish these things, bringing them into fulfillment.

"So shall My word that goes forth from My mouth; it shall not return to Me void, but it shall accomplish what I please, and it shall prosper in the things for which I sent it" (Isaiah 55:11). The devil doesn't know the times and the seasons, and you can see the evidence of that in the Bible as he tried to take out Moses, Noah, and then Jesus multiple times, but he failed.

Jesus showed me that satan orchestrated with willing people to legalize abortion with the intention of taking out this prophetic generation. Still, he missed it again because Jesus told me, as I was standing three feet away from Him, that from now on, every child that comes out of the womb is a prophetic voice. Jesus also said to me, "I know you will make a way for the prophetic words I have given them to be heard."

Children do not typically get a television platform to speak from because they haven't written books, and they're not well known. As a result, one of the main projects that Warrior Notes is working on is making a way for children to release their voices and prophesy. We'll treat them like adults, and we'll train them to prophesy from the fire of God. We're also going to develop warrior parents so they can share and discuss how they've brought up their children as prophets and prophetesses. Jesus told me that the time is now to begin implementing these projects, so we are obeying Him.

The God of Love Spoke You into Existence

When I was in heaven with Jesus, I stood in the same exact spot where God had spoken me into existence, and I presented myself before Him right there. That will happen to all of us; we will stand before our loving, heavenly Father, in the same spot where He created us and where He spoke us into existence. God is not as some have said or imagined. He has not done all these terrible things that have happened to us. In heaven, we will realize that the Holy Spirit was here all along to show us and help us discern between good and evil so that we can avoid satan's plans.

Most people will not find this out until they get to heaven, but why wait? Why not realize now and walk in the truth that your heavenly Father loves you and He never intended these traumatic events to happen to you? The god of this world is bent on terrorism and destruction, and we are to stop him. We are to proclaim the year of the Lord's liberty. (See Luke 4:18.) We are to heal the sick, raise the dead, and drive out devils. We are to proclaim Jubilee, the forgiveness of debt.

You Are the Currency of Heaven

Did you know that there is no money in heaven? This is because *you* are the currency of heaven. You are the most valuable commodity in heaven because you cost the most. Your heavenly Father poured everything into you, and no one else will ever fully appreciate you for what you're worth. No one else will pay you for what you're worth as He has.

> *"Our demand is the catalyst that causes the covenant to kick in for us."*

Jesus showed me that the monetary system down here has been rigged against you. He said to me, "Because you are my child, someone else has your money." Plenty of money is out there, and the devil doesn't want you to have it. Well, what should we do about this? Matthew 7:7 says, "Ask, and it shall be given to you, seek and you shall find, knock and the door shall be opened unto to you."

We don't have to beg or ask God for something that's already ours. God wrote the covenant, and He knows all that's in there. When you place a demand on what is yours, you are actually demanding it from the one who is withholding it from you, which is not God. So when you need healing, you demand your healing to manifest because it's part of the covenant. Our demand is the catalyst that causes the covenant to kick in for us. God said, "You're my child, and here are your adoption papers, and here is the covenant, and everything I have is yours." Are you starting to see what I saw on the other side about how wrong we have gotten it down here?

An Acceleration Must Occur in the Body of Christ

The times and seasons of God are cyclical, along with cycles of revelation. The Spirit of God is with us; however, He moves in cycles. When I was with Jesus, He showed me that the body is behind the curve, so an acceleration must occur. With the acceleration, you'll encounter visitation, and the angels will visit your house, and you will ask, "Why are you favoring me?"

And the angel won't even know. They'll say, "The Lord God sent me." They will come because they've been told to.

> *"Jesus said to me, 'At the end of the age, I will take all the tears of the saints and turn them into wine.'"*

During my visit to heaven, Jesus told me that the last move of God would be *the move of the glory of the Father.* He said, "The Father has reserved the last move for Himself. The last miracle on earth will be the first miracle that I did when I turned water into wine. At the end of the age, I will take all the tears of the saints and turn them into wine." We will experience such amazing joy that we will laugh our way out of here. While we are on earth, seeing the manifestation of God's glory, we won't merely sip the wine. We'll have one of those backpacks with a straw. We will walk in the Spirit, and we may not be sober too often. I can tolerate a lot more when I'm drunk in the Spirit.

When you walk in the Spirit and in freedom, you can go out and tell your friends. Then your friends will encounter and walk in freedom. They will go out and talk to seven other friends, and they, too, will encounter that freedom. This life can be fun, but fun will eventually go away. I want to be full of joy because joy is from the other realm as it's a fruit of the Spirit. Happiness and fun are temporal and based on experiences, but joy is forever because it's spiritual. From now on, we will be full of joy because this is the season for it.

The Equation Is Stacked in Your Favor

When you appear before the Lord at the spot where God spoke your life into existence, you will realize that everything you needed for life and godliness was given to you through the precious promises and that you were a partaker of the divine nature (2 Peter 1:3–4). You will have a clear revelation of whether you had added to your faith all those virtues; you will not be able to fail even if you try. Here is what Jesus told me. He said that with any life failure you could ever possibly go through, your heavenly Father has already put what is necessary into the equation so that you make it. Do you understand what I'm saying? He showed me where He left space, even if we thought we knew more than He does and we got off track. He has already factored all of that into the equation as if you did nothing wrong. When Romans 8:28 says, "He causes all things to work for good to those who love God, to those we are called according to His purpose," it means just that. I know that none of us ever plan on failing, but you need to know that God was never caught off guard by what happened.

If you ever happen to find yourself off track, you can choose to turn back to Jesus and get back on course because the body of Christ needs you. We need you to be on track. I mean, each of us is a part of the same body, right? When one suffers, we all suffer; when one of us becomes crazy for Jesus, we all benefit, right? And I don't know about you, but I need radical, crazy friends for Jesus, ones who are righteous and on fire for God.

It's Not about the Quantity but the Quality

When I died and went to heaven at thirty-one years of age, Jesus explained to me that I had completed everything that He had asked me to do. I asked, "What about my goal of living to one hundred and twenty years on earth?"

Jesus said to me, "It's not the quantity. It's the quality, and you always obeyed me." Jesus told me that He equated faith with obedience. He said, "Even as a little boy, when I spoke to you, you dropped what you were doing, and you didn't question me. You did whatever I asked of you, and because of this, you are well-known in heaven."

I said to Him, "Well, that's what you do."

He replied, "Well, that's rare on earth." It really touched me that people in heaven know about our lives by our obedience.

Jesus Revealed the Whole Game Plan to Me

As Jesus spoke to me, I thought, *Is this really happening?* I mean, here's Jesus, talking to me about the greatest move and the greatest harvest yet to come. While He was talking to me, Boaz came over to talk with me too. Boaz is a small Jewish man with these little curls in his hair, but when I met him, I knew that he was very wealthy while he was on earth. Boaz proceeded to teach me about the Kinsman Redeemer. Jesus wants me to release this message here on earth because our heavenly Father wants you to know about this as well. It's time for Him to love on you. You must know He has redeemed you, but the time is now for the show to begin because He will reveal His glory to the world, and He will use us, His children.

Jesus showed me how Enoch walked so closely with God. He followed God, and he went out and prophesied repentance to all those cities. Enoch wasn't hiding in a cave watching end-time DVDs about the antichrist while eating rice and beans. He was about his Father's business. I saw this, and I saw him take his last step on earth. I also saw Elijah get into the chariot as a whirlwind of fire surrounded him. These men were meant to go out and do the work of the Lord. They were not to hide, and God made sure they weren't hiding somewhere in a cave. We won't make the mistake of staying hidden in these last days, will we?

> *"God needs us to be mature Christians on the earth right now because that's what's needed for this time and season."*

What will it look like as we go out and minister to others in these last days? Ministry happens through the fivefold as intended by God to build up the body of believers. Ministry also happens in our everyday lives in the marketplace. I used to minister to people at my job when I worked at Southwest Airlines; however, now I reach people through various other methods as I always focus on prophesying and building up the body of Christ. I want to get believers off the bottle and Pampers. I want believers to start asking, "Where's the beef?"

God needs us to be mature Christians on earth right now because it's required for this time and season. In May 2020, Jesus had to walk me through Ephesians 4, explaining what His intention has always been for the fivefold ministry in the body of Christ, and then I saw how we had missed it. This was very hard for me as I've been to two Bible schools and been to heaven, but He still had to walk me through this so that I would see and understand. It hit me so hard that I couldn't even talk, which was what I needed because I already know what I know, and I just wanted to listen and hear everything that Jesus had to say. There is fantastic news, though! We will come back with Him—I saw this. It has already been set in motion.

God expects you to fulfill what He has written about you in your books in heaven. Yes, I talk about this all the time because I want people to know about their book in heaven. I realize that so many have not been made aware that Psalm 139 even exists, let alone that God had spoken over their life when they were in their mother's womb. On that day, God wrote out all the details of each of our lives, and I want people to know this wonderful truth and the fact that God only sees you making it.

God's Favor Poured Out on Us

No one even bothers to come to me about abortion because my whole ministry is based on Psalms 139:16. They don't even say a peep about it because they know what they're going to get. This is how I live: I let people know what I believe, and then they will only gingerly approach me because they already know where I stand. They will think, *Why even go there*? The truth is already out there, so there is no story or news flash. What we stand for is already clear. So as you live this way, just watch what happens with the favor of the Lord in your life.

Jesus explained to me that God's favor is released on us when the Father smiles at you, and the beams of the glory coming from His face hit you. He sits back and starts laughing in expectation of all the amazing things that will start happening in your life. I'm not kidding you about this, and I can't even oversimplify it. God smiles at you, and then it's jubilee. It won't be fair to your enemies because they will think, *You've got to be kidding me.* Your debts will be canceled; it will be so unbelievable, and you won't be able to explain it.

> *"Do whatever you can for someone and do it for a person you know could never pay you back as it positions you so that only God can pay you back."*

I really want you to take hold of this. You need to continue working and being diligent, doing everything you can. If He tells you to invest, you invest. If you don't know what to invest in, just find an orphan, a widow, a child, or a single parent and give to them. I don't care if it's a can of beans. Do whatever you can for someone and do it for a person you know could never pay you back as it positions you so that only God can pay you back. Just try it and watch and see what happens. My wife and I do this all the time, and because of this, something supernatural happens for us every day. Just ask my staff. It occurs daily in our lives because we've chosen not to do this ourselves.

This Is God's Show, Not Mine

My students ask me all the time, "How can I practice the presence of God?"

I will tell you the secret that Jesus said to me, "My next exhale is your inhale." It's mouth-to-mouth, and I'm telling you, there's nothing like the breath of Jesus. I mean, Jesus is life. His words are Spirit, and His words are life. (See John 6:63.) Can you even imagine God giving you mouth-to-mouth resuscitation? But see, to me, He does it every day. Why? Because on the other side, I couldn't get back into my body when I died. I couldn't save myself. I couldn't bring myself back unless He gave the command for my spirit to return to my body. That is why I stay humble. I know I have no control, and it's not my show. My show is on my back porch with my wife in retirement, drinking unsweetened tea. That's my gig.

Jesus told me that this is the time and the season for nobodies to come forth. He's calling people that no one knows, but He knows them. Jesus told me that if the adults don't do it, the children will. He spoke to me about the Father's plan for the children, so I'm getting ready because I've met these kids.

Do you want to become humble really quickly? Just give a microphone to a child who has the power of God in their lives, and when they start prophesying, all of a sudden, you just want to go home and read your Bible.

No More Idle Words

When Jesus appeared to me, one of the first things He talked about was the words I had spoken. He leaned in toward me, and He said, "You'll be held accountable for every idle word that comes out of your mouth." And then he looked directly at me, and He said, "I meant that." I knew very clearly that He was serious. Then Jesus explained to me that He and His Father chose to bring all creation into existence through their words. Even the laws set in motion that we encounter on earth, such as gravity, were all brought into existence through their words. Think about it: The Father and the Son spoke everything into existence. Their words continue, even though we are in a fallen state. Adam still lived 930 years outside the garden. That shows you how much life was in that man. All those people continued to live for hundreds of years, even after the fall.

Our generation will likely live to be eighty or ninety years of age, but what if the times and seasons change and God allows us to live even longer? What if it's about to change so that the doctors will be scratching their heads, wondering what's going on? Jesus told me, "If I want this generation to live longer to fulfill prophecy, then I will do it." And He doesn't even have to get up off his throne to make that happen. He just speaks the word, giving the command.

We are His children, and we are in His house; we are His family. We don't have to knock or set up an appointment to enter, we're already in, and Jesus said that we have been given authority to speak to a mountain, directing it where to go, and it will obey us if we believe and do not doubt in our hearts (Mark 11:23). Those words are in red; He said that this is the way the Father set this up. I'm teaching you the truth about how we're supposed to operate. We must learn to watch our words. Jesus said to me, "Kevin, the body of Christ should only be speaking their destination, only talking about where they are going."

God Has Established Everything That Is Yours

In heaven, Jesus took me and showed me all the different things that I own, like my car, all my keyboards and instruments, anything I own with a serial number on it. He told me that as people were assembling my car; it was already my car. When the man in China assembled my cello, he was doing that especially for me, even before he knew it. Heaven foreknew every little thing that would be mine before those things were ever made. Even though the people who made those things might not have known God, they were doing God's work and didn't even realize it. It was all being done for me. Are you getting this? Someone made the seat you are sitting in right now. The person that made it might not have even wanted to work that day, but God knew that someday you would require that item to be at the place you are now, learning about all these great truths and the good news regarding your heavenly Father.

When Kathi and I bought our first camera, we had to work extra hours at our jobs to pay for it. But that serial number on there had always been designated as part of Warrior Notes. At times, God told us to give specific cameras to churches, so God already knew what would happen—those particular cameras would be designated to those churches.

A Manifestation of Faith

> *"Stay out of your head, go down into your spirit, and receive what God has for you."*

What mountain do you need to speak to right now? Jesus said that if you speak to the mountain, believing from your heart and not from your head, you will have what you ask for. Faith is not a head exercise; faith is of the heart. Your spirit is lit up, and you've been given your portion of faith. You just need to use it, believing as a child. Stay out of your head, go down into your spirit, and receive what God has for you. Right now, as you are reading these truths, God knows those who have ears to hear and those who will take this revelation and put it into motion because Jesus loves manifestation.

The Lord showed me that some people reading this book have been holding onto unforgiveness. The Lord wants you to release forgiveness; just let those people go. That person is not going to get away with anything they have done. Yes, release forgiveness now. Hand the case file over to Jesus and receive healing in your body, and then as you stand speaking to your mountain, believing with your heart and staying out of your head, receive as a child receives. This is your day. As I write this, I see the prophet Joel spinning around in heaven, dancing right now.

The Time and Season for Manifestation Is Now

Now is the time and season for manifestation to happen in all the churches for all believers, but it's not fully manifesting yet because many are thinking, *If we can just hold on until he comes.* Or *If I could just pay my bills next month.* We've gotten ourselves into this compromised position because we have been traumatized by this world system, but we must understand that we're not *of* this world system. So we have to separate ourselves and come out from among them (2 Corinthians 6:17). We do that by discerning and knowing that our heavenly Father can take care of us. We trust Him, and when we do, He starts to manifest His goodness to us. He shows us His goodness, and then we repent. After we repent, we walk with Him.

If you experience feelings or thoughts that you haven't measured up, all you need to do is look at the blood of Jesus that poured down His body and is always present at the mercy seat. Jesus is sitting right next to the Father on the mercy seat. Those cherubim are real; they're not gold, and He is seated on top of the ark of the covenant (Hebrews 9:23–24). It's God's throne, and those cherubim are huge, and the blood has been applied, once and for all.

We cannot go by feelings because the blood speaks, and blood has a voice, right? Isn't that what God said to Cain when he killed Abel? He came down and said, "What have you done? The voice of your brother's blood cries out to Me from the ground" (Genesis 4:10). Can you imagine then how loud Jesus's blood is? It's speaking right now, and it's speaking things about you. Jesus's blood is speaking as though you have never sinned or messed up. If Jesus appears to you, He's not going to know what you're talking about as you go through your past stories; no, you don't have to go through all that. Jesus is saying that you have no history; it's gone. Paul said, "I've wronged no man," and Stephen said, "Excuse me, I think you killed me." But God sees us as blameless even when we know we have done something we shouldn't have. Paul also said, "I was appointed as an apostle since birth." Excuse me, wasn't he knocked down on the Damascus Road? Wasn't he being stupid like the rest of us until he met Jesus on that road?

The Time Is Now to Walk in Your Authority

Barney Fife wouldn't hesitate to give out a ticket to someone just for looking at him funny. Why? Because he took it as though you were disrespecting him. He would arrest people just based on suspicion. Some won't know how to take you when you begin walking in your authority. When they hear you, they will notice you are different. Look at what happened when people first heard Jesus speak; they recognized that He spoke with authority and that He was different from the teachers of the law (Matthew 7:28–29). As people heard the truth spoken with authority, the demons that had entrenched themselves in the people became nervous. When Jesus came on the scene, a lot of lawlessness was being permitted, and the demons began manifesting when Jesus spoke.

In May 2020, Jesus showed me that if the body of Christ did not begin walking in their authority, that the lawlessness we had been experiencing earlier in the year would become much worse by the coming September. I saw cities on fire and troops occupying various cities, but Jesus told me that if the church prayed and walked in their authority, we could change history. See what happens when you are anointed, appointed, and chosen, which you are? Demons will not know how to deal with you because it will be as if they're dealing with a brand-new breed. They're used to Christians operating in lukewarmness and compromise. You may be wondering what lukewarmness looks like. It looks like demons sitting on the front row at church, listening to some of the songs, the ones that talk about God but never talk to Him. The demons love some of those songs.

> *"Those who are on fire for Jesus know that it's all about relationship."*

A church on fire for God will know that Jesus is right there with them because Matthew 18:20 says, "For where two or three are gathered together in My name, I am there in the midst of them." Those Christians who are gathered will know that they are singing to Jesus, not just about Him—that's how worship looks. If we're merely singing about God and never to Him, we are just informing people with facts.

However, those on fire for Jesus know that it's all about relationship.

What happens when a Christian approaches one of those loudmouthed legislators who have been in politics for forty-seven years, the ones that no one knows how they have gotten re-elected? What happens when an on-fire Christian comes on the scene, walking in the power of God? Those legislators won't even be able to talk. They won't be able to say a word, and then that believer will start prophesying. It will be you, walking in the power of God. As people encounter you walking in your authority, they will have to get rid of their invisible friends. The demons will leave, and then suddenly, they won't have the power or influence on the people they used to. I'm telling you the truth; this is what we can do even from our own houses as we pray. We can stop the power behind the evil.

The Lukewarm Church

In these times and seasons and in this current dispensation, Jesus is releasing the fire but not in lukewarm organizations. If you're part of the fivefold ministry and you're speaking from the fire, I want to go to church there because I want to be built up. I know people that prefer to go to the lake on their boat on Sunday instead of going to church. The draw is not because they have a new engine on their boat or they just got the latest fishing gear. No, it's because they want to be somewhere else. After all, at least if they're on the lake, they're having fun.

When they go to church, they get nothing. If they experienced church and encountered the presence and the fire of God, they would want to be there. I would trade being on a lake on a boat with being in an on-fire church any day! You would even pay with a pearl of great price to be in a house where God was present and dwelling; you would quickly sell everything you had (Matthew 13:45). However, if you're going to sit there and sing "Kumbaya" with a three-string guitar and only hope that He comes by, I'm sorry, it's not going to happen. Can you see how we've gotten ourselves into this situation? We've gotten ourselves into a lukewarm state.

In the wilderness, God gave the children of Israel another chance after they rejected Him; Moses built the tabernacle and the tent of meeting, and guess who showed up to that meeting? Only Moses and Joshua, no one else. The people—

all of Israel—came out of their tents and watched Moses and Joshua go into the tent of meeting because the pillar of fire and cloud of glory came onto the tent. But none of them went in; that is where we're at right now. We would rather have someone else do it for us, carry us, or pray for us instead of praying for ourselves. The last time I checked, the Holy Spirit was a Counselor; we can go directly to Him.

Your Designated Times and Seasons

When you're flying an airplane, you need to begin adjusting the plane in advance in preparation to land at your intended destination. In order to do this, you have to know your exact speed and distance from the landing strip so that you can start coordinating your descent. You can't wait to begin adjusting your speed just seven miles away and expect to land the plane at your planned target. If you did that, you would miss the entire state. That may be okay if you're by yourself, but usually, you're not. More than likely, some people on the plane will be mad at you. They would say, "I thought you were a pilot."

Flying a plane requires constant managing and thinking ahead. That's what the Holy Spirit would say to you if you were trying to land without Him. "That's why you're where you are at this time. You didn't manage your approach with Me but tried to do it without me. Why didn't you give me the controls when you were about to crash?" God has specific destinations planned in our lives because there are times and seasons for us from the Lord, and He knows how to interpret those times and seasons. If we yield to His leading, He will guide us, ensuring that we do not miss our appointed times.

The Missing Stone in Hillel's Breastplate

Did you know the word "lucifer" isn't actually used for the name of satan in the Hebrew translation of the Bible? His name has been interpreted that way, but the original word is *hillel* in Hebrew, which means "bright and shiny one."[5] Hillel was only given nine stones, not the twelve given to the priest in his breastplate (Ezekiel 28:13–14, 17–20). When I discovered that, I wanted to find out what stones he wasn't given because I know that God does everything intentionally.

---

[5] "Lexicon :: Strong's H1985 – hillēl," *Blue Letter Bible*, accessed September 17, 2021, https://www.blueletterbible.org/lexicon/h1985/kjv/wlc/0-1/.

Once I saw that God left out three stones, I thought even in our government, we compartmentalize everything for security reasons, and that way, no one person has all the information or power. I know friends currently working on classified aircraft, and people won't even know about it for twenty or thirty years. Each person working on their own section has no idea what the entire final aircraft or spacecraft will look like, which is as it should be because if other countries were to get ahold of that piece, they wouldn't know either. So God, in His infinite wisdom, already knew that *hillel* would rebel and take one-third of the angels with him. One of the three stones that He left out of his breastplate was the stone of Issachar, which is the anointing to know the times and the seasons (1 Chronicles 12:32). He does not know the times and seasons, which is precisely why he missed Moses, Noah, and Jesus, and now he's missed an entire prophetic generation.

Jesus Is the Only Mediator Between God and Man

"It's a great deception if we think we're holding out until Jesus comes."

While Christians are so focused on trying to figure out who the antichrist is, calculating the number of his name, Jesus told me that in every generation, satan has groomed a person, preparing them to step in as the antichrist because he doesn't know the timing of God. So now it's delayed, and the son of perdition will not be revealed. Once again, he will die unseated, and it won't happen until God says it's time. So what should Christians do in the meantime? We are to rise and be who we were called to be. We begin owning everything.

I don't need a middleman because there's only one mediator between God and man, and it isn't any of us, and the last time I checked, it's not even the pope. It's Jesus. Small wars have been fought over this; denominations have come and gone because they've tried to take the place of the Counselor. Those who the Spirit of God leads are called the sons of God, not the fivefold ministry. This is the elephant in the room that most churches don't want to address.

Watch what happens. Everything you're worried about will just disappear because this happens all the time. Every generation thinks the end is coming. People have believed that for two thousand years. In Thessalonica, Paul had to say, "You don't eat if you don't work, so go back to work." They had quit their jobs and were on their rooftops. Paul had to tell the Thessalonians that it was not time for the end and then explained what would happen before Christ's return. He explained about the son of perdition and how he was being held back from coming (2 Thessalonians 2). He doesn't say who is holding him back, but we know it's the Holy Spirit through the church. Christ will not come back while we're here, so it's a great deception if we think we're holding out until Jesus comes.

It's Time to Give God the Controls

God's Spirit reveals the times and the seasons of the Lord, but satan is not in on this information. He had to try and use other people to figure it out for him, people like Herod or Pharaoh. At some point, we just need to put it down and say to God, "You know what? You can have the controls. You started this, and You can finish it because You're the author and finisher of my faith. I know I cannot fail in Your hands, even though the circumstances may be screaming otherwise."

One day, when I was in flight training school, I started experiencing turbulence and couldn't keep the airplane in alignment. I was so busy focusing on the turbulence and keeping the plane flying that a few moments later, I hadn't realized the turbulence had subsided, and the autopilot had taken over and brought us into complete alignment. Because I hadn't realized we had come out of the turbulence, I still tried to keep the plane in alignment myself, essentially shadowboxing when I didn't need to. My instructor explained that I just needed to let go of the controls because the plane could do a better job than I could.

I'm telling you this story because the Spirit of the Lord wants you to know that we can become so fixated on the problem that we don't know when the problem has actually subsided. This is why you have to discern the times and the seasons and know when it's time to let go of the controls and hand it over to Him. Even the instructor knew he didn't need to grab the yoke or the throttle when I let go because the autopilot would bring us into a perfectly smooth and level flight. God is showing me that this happened to some of you reading this book. Satan brought some traumatic events into your life, and you're still trying to fight. Still, the truth is that He has already left the room because God has brought you everything you need; you just need to receive it.

God's Movement Is Beyond What You Can See

The Lord is asking me to share another story with you. After I met Jesse Duplantis, the Lord told him one day, "Kevin is for real, and the world needs to hear his story." Now Kathi and I hadn't approached Jesse, asking for anything. All we had been doing was fasting and praying.

One day, Jesse called me and said, "I have called Jan Crouch, and I'm going to interview you on TBN."

I asked Jesse, "How did this happen?"

He said, "You didn't bother me or ask me for anything, and the Lord showed me you and Kathi in your prayer closet." I couldn't believe it; after Jesse interviewed us on TBN, our ministry launched. TBN had so many people calling in to accept Christ and so much fruit resulted from me sharing my story. Jesse said to me, "This is what you were made for."

The day after the interview, Kathi and I got up at four o'clock in the morning and started praying in tongues. We prayed for about four hours, but we weren't breaking through in the Spirit like we usually would. We thought this was impossible; we had prayed for four hours, had three cups of tea, and nothing. I then said to Kathi, "Something is going on here. Let's take a break and back off." While we were taking a break, I decided to go to the hot tub and thought, *I'll just wait on the Lord.* As I reached that in-between state of being awake and fully asleep, my head fell forward, and I saw four angels standing there, staring at me. Immediately, I woke up and looked around but didn't see anything. Right then, I could feel the power of God in my spirit so strong, but in my mind, I couldn't sense anything. I started feeling depressed, and I don't normally ever feel depressed. I thought, *Something is wrong here.* A few minutes later, I fell asleep again, and when I did, those four angels were standing there, smiling at me. I then heard them speak to me and say, "Get up! Get dressed and get ready. Hurry, you only have one hour."

I woke up and said to Kathi, "Get ready, we have to leave within one hour." I'm telling you this story because you need to know that what you may be feeling or experiencing can be the total opposite of what's really going on in the spirit; satan will try to hide what God is doing.

By the time Kathi and I had gotten ready, Jesse called me and said, "Can you meet me at the jet because the Lord is telling me that you need to go to Del Way's church?" This all happened within an hour of my experience with the feelings of depression. Three weeks before my interview on TBN, I had been in my house with Jesse's magazine sitting on a table, and I opened it and saw an article about Jesse going to visit the church of the Christian singer, Del Way. When I saw it, I said, "Lord, I really love Del Way, and one day I would like to go to his church." Mark 11:24 tells us that whatever we ask for, if we believe that we receive, we will have it. After praying that prayer a few weeks prior, I had a dream about being in his church, and an angel took me all around, building by building, so I knew in detail where everything was at this church; I knew the whole layout.

Once we arrived at the church with Jesse, I didn't need anyone to show me around or where to go; I already knew from my dream. So this is what I want you to see. The four angels knew that this was supposed to happen, and they were sent to make sure that we were ready. They were so bright, full of light, and smiling so happily. I know this is a very personal story, but I'm writing about it for you to know that what you're experiencing in this realm might not be anything close to what's about to happen for you. When I met Del Way, it was such a blessing for me, and to think just before this happened, Kathi and I had been praying in the Spirit for four hours, seemingly not getting anywhere. We all experience war here, but all along, something is happening in the Spirit. Those angels were assigned to me because I was feeling depressed, but I had no reason to be, so they made sure I got ready to make it to where I needed to go.

Jesse pulled me aside and asked, "Do you realize what is happening to you?"

I said, "No."

Then he said, "You have nothing to worry about. Everything is already taken care of for you. What has happened to you in the past year would normally take people over forty years in ministry to accomplish."

It's all about the times and seasons of the Lord, and He determines all these things beforehand. Satan is left out of it. But if he sees four angels standing beside you, he's figuring that something's about to happen. Each of us is part of what God is doing on the earth. You just haven't been informed yet, but activity around you would dictate that something's going on. Otherwise, you wouldn't even be reading this book or pursuing the things of God.

"But God now unveils these profound realities to us by the Spirit. Yes, he has revealed to us his inmost heart and deepest mysteries through the Holy Spirit, who constantly explores all things" (1 Corinthians 2:10 TPT). Paul said that the Spirit of God searches the deep things of God, and He reveals them to us, and we can understand them because we have the mind of Christ (1 Corinthians 2:16). You don't hear this part quoted very often. God desires to reveal secrets from His inmost heart and deepest mysteries because "no eye has seen, no ear has heard, and no mind has imagined what God has prepared for those who love him" (1 Corinthians 2:9 NLT). What Paul said in 1 Corinthians 2:10 supersedes the idea that we don't understand the times and seasons because now we do; the deep mysteries of Christ have been revealed to us.

Give It All to God and See What Happens

Right now, as I am releasing this message, I am on the sapphire floor in heaven, and God is showing me some things for you. Take out a blank sheet of paper and write down everything in your possession: your ministry, family, businesses, jobs, friends, everything that God shows you. If you lay it down and give it all to Him, He will give you such a great measure of wisdom in all those areas. God has shown me that there is an open heaven, and this is the season for your heavenly Father to bring manifestation and wisdom in all those areas of your life. If you ask Him, He will also help you write out your vision that you don't have yet but that you know He has purposed for you to have.

The Lord recently showed me that I need to shift my schedule as He began revealing all these programs to me. One of these is Warrior Fellowship, where people will have Bible Studies in their homes all over the world. We have been writing the curriculum and providing what people need to launch and hold gatherings to come together with other believers in their homes and communities to study the Word.

The Lord has shown me that this is the time and season to give it all to Him and see what happens. As you do, He will begin to explain things to you and bring you answers. I know I want to listen to my heavenly Father just as Jesus did. I want to go where He tells me to go and say what He tells me to say (John 5:19).

Now Is the Time for the Church to Shine

God is showing me that He wants to bring this to your house. He wants to establish that if the devil ever has another lame idea about keeping you locked up in your home, he will regret it for the rest of eternity, which happens to be a very long time. The devil will think, *Why did I just do that? Why did I keep them locked up in their houses? Now they're having church in their houses, and angels are showing up. Their kids are prophesying when they wake up. They're washing their own Sippy cups and cleaning their rooms because angels are there.*

You are here on earth right now, and you're reading this message because it's your time. It's time for the church to shine. Some people are afraid to be the leader that God created them to be, so we need to help them. We need to encourage our pastors and leaders, but we also need to do what we can ourselves. You can build yourself up in the Holy Spirit by praying in tongues, and you can meditate on the Word of God. You can stand up as the new sheriff in town, make declarations, and give out commands. Let's all do this and see what happens.

God Is in the Details

Those of you that have had God place a desire in you to start your own business need to begin planning your next steps. Begin by creating your graphics, praying, and mapping out exactly who you want to be involved in your business. Write down their names and then place the entire plan before the Lord. Once you start, God will give you His ideas. He will show other people what they need to do to help you have the product and services ready to go. He will cause you to anticipate people's needs before they come, and this is how He will make you successful. Jesus said to me, "I will give people ideas, anticipating the needs that others have, and I will cause them to meet those needs."

> *"The Lord plants the gifts in you, and then He makes a demand for those gifts from other people."*

God has placed the gift inside you, and then He puts the demand around you, and your value goes through the roof. Are you hearing and receiving what I'm saying? The Lord plants the gifts in you, and then He makes a demand for those gifts from other people. It's all rigged in your favor, and you will succeed when you believe with all your heart, not doubting; God is with you in a powerful way. This was already set in motion long before you were born. It was predetermined that if you would believe and obey, nothing would be impossible to you (Mark 9:23).

Jesus Wants Your Soul Healed

The Lord is also letting me know that many of you reading this right now have wounds in your soul that need to be healed. These wounds may have happened due to words or curses spoken over you when you were an impressionable child. He just reminded me of the damage I used to have in my soul, which warped my thinking. The Lord is telling me to share my experience on the operating table with Him. As I was standing next to Jesus, I looked down and saw myself on the operating table; Jesus revealed to me in the spirit that a black vest was on me. It started from my stomach area and went up to my throat. He said it was there because of words and curses that had been spoken over me.

Then He said, "Kevin, I can heal those kinds of scars in four ways. First, I could come in the night and take my hand over a person and just pull the black vest off them. Second, a person can meditate on the Word of God, and the goodness of God, and that will transform and renew their mind, allowing their spirit to become dominant. Third, according to Jude 1:20, you could build your spirit up on your most holy faith by praying in the Holy Spirit and keeping yourself in the love of God. When you do this, your spirit goes into overdrive. It will take their mind and pin it down and make it listen. Lastly, you could receive godly counsel from someone who can walk you through healing." But Jesus went on to explain that "what is most important is that you allow your soul to be dominated by your spirit, staying in the love of God, and building up your spirit in the most holy faith."

Don't Stop—Breakthrough Is Here!

I have people ask me how they can get their souls healed. They have shared with me that the Lord will have them repeat a specific phrase in the Spirit; however, they can't seem to move beyond that phrase. The Lord showed me that's because the Spirit is reinforcing something at the specific place, and He's pounding away at it like a hammer until it's broken, so you will repeat something because your spirit is reinforcing that. If you continue to do that, you will break through, and then you will go to other phrases with a fluency. I tell you this to encourage you. Don't be discouraged if you are not fluent in your prayer language at this time. You're in a battle, and there's a partition between your soul and spirit that only the Word of God can separate. It divides between the two.

Jesse Duplantis once asked me, "What do you want?" And I told him that I wanted what was in my spirit. I wanted a school, to be on television and media, and to have my own studio. I wanted to write books and hold big conferences so that I could disciple people. So every week, Jesse prayed over that list with us when we were together. In early 2018, I had six partners. We wrote everything out on a piece of paper, and now it is in our possession, and it's all happening. In mid-2021, as I am writing this, we have nine thousand people partnering with our ministry. And just think, all this happened for a flight attendant and a hairdresser. So what can God do for you, and what does He want to do through you? You can change history. All you need to do is sit in His presence and let Him speak to you. He will talk to you right now.

SALVATION PRAYER

Lord God,
I confess that I am a sinner.
I confess that I need your Son, Jesus.
Please forgive me in His name.
Lord Jesus, I believe You died for me and that you are
alive and listening to me now.
I now turn from my sins and welcome you
into my heart. Come and take control of my life.
Make me the kind of person You want me to be.
Now, fill me with your Holy Spirit, who will show me
how to live for You. I acknowledge You before men as
my Savior and my Lord.
In Jesus's name. Amen.

If you prayed this prayer, please contact us at
info@kevinzadai.com for more information and
material. Go to www.KevinZadai.com for other
exciting ministry materials.

We welcome you to join our network at
Warriornotes.tv. Join our ministry and training school
at Warrior Notes School of Ministry.

Visit KevinZadai.com for more info.

ABOUT DR. KEVIN L. ZADAI

Kevin Zadai ThD was called to the ministry at the age of ten. He attended Central Bible College in Springfield, Missouri, where he received a bachelor of arts in theology. Later, he received training in missions at Rhema Bible College and a doctorate of theology from Primus University. He is currently ordained through Rev. Dr. Jesse and Rev. Dr. Cathy Duplantis.

At the age of thirty-one, during a routine day surgery, he found himself "on the other side of the veil" with Jesus. For forty-five minutes, the Master revealed spiritual truths before returning him to his body and assigning him to a supernatural ministry.

Kevin holds a commercial pilot license and is retired from Southwest Airlines after twenty-nine years as a flight attendant. Kevin is the founder and president of Warrior Notes School of Ministry. He and his lovely wife, Kathi, reside in New Orleans, Louisiana.

Other Books and Study Guides by Dr. Kevin L. Zadai

Kevin has written over fifty books and study guides
Please see our website at www.Kevinzadai.com for a
complete list of materials!

A Meeting Place with God,
The Heavenly Encounters
Series Volume 1

The Heavenly Encounters
Series Volume 1

The Agenda of Angels

The Agenda of Angels
Study Guide

Days of Heaven on Earth

Days of Heaven on Earth:
A Study Guide to the Days
Ahead

Days of Heaven on Earth
Prayer and Confession Guide

Encountering the Heavenly
Sapphire Devotional

Encountering the Heavenly
Sapphire Study Guide:

Encountering God's Will

Encountering God's
Normal Study Guide

From Breakthrough to
Overthrow Study Guide

Have you Been to
the Altar Lately?

Healing Devotional

Heavenly Visitation

Heavenly Visitation: A Study
Guide to Participating in the
Supernatural

Heavenly Visitation
Prayer and Confession Guide

How to Minister to the Sick
Study Guide

It's Rigged in Your Favor

Study Guide: It's all
Rigged in Your Favor

*It's Time to Take
Back our Country*

*Lord Help Me to Understand
Myself Study Guide*

Mystery of the Power Words

*Mystery of the Power Words
Study Guide*

*Praying From the
Heavenly Realms*

*Praying From the Heavenly
Realms Study Guide*

Receiving from Heaven

*Receiving From Heaven
Study Guide*

*Stories From the Glory with
Sister Ruth Carneal*

Supernatural Finances

*Supernatural Finances
Study Guide*

*Supernatural Finances
Devotional*

*Supernatural Prayer
Strategies of a Warrior*

*Taking a Stand
Against the Enemy*

Taking off the Limitations

*Taking off the Limitations
Study Guide*

*The Vision and Battle
Strategies of Warrior Notes
Intl.*

*Notes of a Warrior: The
Secrets of Spiritual Warfare
Volume 1 Study Guide*

*Notes of a Warrior: The
Secrets of Spiritual Warfare
Volume 2 Study Guide*

You Can Hear God's Voice

*You Can Hear God's Voice
Study Guide*

*Your Hidden Destiny
Revealed, The Heavenly
Encounters Series Volume 2*

*Praying From the Heavenly
Realms Study Guide*

*Warrior Fellowships Season 1
Volume 1 Study Guide*

*Warrior Fellowships Season 1
Volume 2 Study Guide*

*Warrior Notes Aviation
Volume 1: Flight Manual
Study Guide*

Warrior Women
Volume 1 Study Guide

Warrior Women
Volume 2 Study Guide

Warrior Justice: A Study
Guide to Experiencing
Freedom from Demonic
Oppression

Made in the USA
Monee, IL
18 October 2021

8e0e9398-aef8-4abc-9580-40b6307b28ddR01